A fascinatingly anecdotal introduction to the practice of solitary retreat, encouraging us to go often and alone into the wild. – **Kamalashila**, author of *Buddhist Meditation: Tranquillity, Imagination and Insight*

This is a seriously beautiful book – beautiful writing about beautiful places – and a wise one too. With its practical good sense, lack of self-indulgence and purity of heart, it will encourage, 'give courage to', those who have longed for but have not dared to try out solitude. It will also deepen the practice of those of us (Buddhist or otherwise, and I am otherwise) who already know the deep joys and freedoms, but also the harsh realities, of solitude in nature, in wildness. It is grounded in authentic knowledge and experience. Get out there – but take *Wild Awake* with you. – **Sara Maitland**, author of *How to Be Alone* and *Gossip from the Forest*

To spend time alone in nature is essential for us to begin to understand what we truly are. This book evokes the quality of those times – the way in which the heart begins to ground itself into the spirit of a place, remembering its own wildness. – **Maitridevi**, Chair of Taraloka Retreat Centre

Vajragupta gives us a wonderful evocation of how to use solitude as a way of deepening our resonance with the natural world. But, even more than that, he shows us how this vivid aliveness to the world leads to 'a quietening of the self' that, paradoxically, leaves us 'saturated with life'. – **Subhadramati**, author of *Not About Being Good*

Wild Awake

Alone, Offline, and Aware in Nature

Vajragupta

Windhorse Publications

Windhorse Publications
169 Mill Road
Cambridge
CB1 3AN
United Kingdom
info@windhorsepublications.com
windhorsepublications.com

Typesetting and layout by Ruth Rudd
Cover design by Bodhikara
Photograph Vajragupta © Suvannamani

Printed by Bell & Bain Ltd, Glasgow

British Library Cataloguing in Publication Data:
A catalogue record for this book is available from the British Library

ISBN: 978-1-911407-18-8

I found in myself, and still find, an instinct toward a higher, or, as it is named, spiritual life ... and another toward a primitive rank and savage one, and I reverence them both. I love the wild not less than the good.

Thoreau[1]

Contents

About the author

Vajragupta was ordained into the Triratna Buddhist Order in 1994. He was director of the Birmingham Buddhist Centre from 1997 to 2005, and director of the European Triratna Development Team (helping support a network of about fifty Buddhist centres across Europe) from 2006 to 2014. These days he lives as a 'wandering Dharma farer' – spending periods of time teaching and helping out at different Buddhist communities around the world, and also making time for writing. *Buddhism: Tools for Living Your Life* was his first book; since then he has written a number of other books on Buddhism. He is currently working on *Free Time*, a book about our relationship with time.

Acknowledgements

Writing is a solitary business; writing this book involved hundreds of hours, hunched all alone, over the keyboard. But I didn't write it by myself; it is the product of many, wide-ranging, influences. All sorts of people were peering over my shoulder offering advice and support.

I would especially like to thank two people – Alan Mahar and Liz Bayley – who very generously read two versions of the text and made comments from which I have learnt a great deal and been able to hugely improve what I wrote. I feel a debt of gratitude to them both.

I would also like to thank the following friends for reading and giving feedback on various drafts, or in other ways offering suggestions and encouragement: Larry Butler, Danasamudra, Dhammadassin, Jayasraddha, Kalyacitta, Kulajalini, Martin Vaughan Lewis, Lokabandhu, Mahasiddhi, Nagamani, Catherine Payne, Prajnabandhu, Shantighosha, Siddhisambhava, Janet Taylor, Vaddhaka, and Vajrajyoti.

Thank you to Vessantara and Vijayamala for a retreat in which we explored the myth of Mucalinda and his meeting with the Buddha. Thank you to Vajrajyoti for her interpretation of the story of the Buddha's encounter with the rampaging elephant. Thanks to Larry Butler for bringing the Thomas A. Clark poem to my attention.

Acknowledgements

As a writer I know just how fortunate I am to have a publisher who understands and sympathizes with what I am trying to write. I feel very grateful to the staff and trustees of Windhorse Publications, especially to Priyananda who has been at the helm at Windhorse for many years now, and to Michelle Bernard, who patiently, carefully, and efficiently guided this book through to publication. I also want to thank Cynthia Troupe who so sensitively and carefully edited the text, Dhatvisvari for her skilled copy-editing, and also Bodhikara for the fine cover design. Thank you Suvannamani for the author photograph.

Lastly, I would like to express my gratitude to those who made available the solitary-retreat facilities that I have stayed in over many years. Having simple and affordable places to stay, in quiet and beautiful locations, is such a blessing. Those places are a precious resource and I, and I know many others, have gained so much from being able to spend time alone in them.

Publisher's acknowledgements

Windhorse Publications wishes to gratefully acknowledge a grant from the Triratna European Chairs' Assembly Fund and the Future Dharma Fund towards the production of this book.

Windhorse Publications also wishes to gratefully acknowledge and thank the individual donors who gave to the book's production via our 'Sponsor-a-book' campaign.

Introduction

Over twenty-five years ago, when I was in my early twenties, I went on my first 'solitary retreat', staying for two weeks in a caravan amongst hills and mountains that rose steeply out of the sea in west Wales. It was a quietly life-changing experience. Nearly every year since then I have made time to get away and be alone. Solitary retreats have become an integral part of my life, and the source of some of my most precious memories. I have discovered a love of solitude, silence, and simplicity. This book tells the story of that discovery and why it still feels so important.

In particular, the book relates how being in nature came to be such an intrinsic part of those solitary retreats. My love for the aliveness of the places I stayed in, and of the creatures that lived there, became increasingly strong and heartfelt. I found that the outer world and my inner world spoke more and more deeply to each other. I had moments in which the barrier that I usually experienced between me and the world was lowered like never before. And, when this happened, so much beauty revealed itself.

Each chapter finds me at a certain phase in my life, spending time at a particular location. That caravan on the peninsula in Wales, a cabin hidden in a mountain valley in southern Spain, a wooden shack on a beach in the Highlands of Scotland, a charming stone cottage in the hill-farming country of Cumbria, an old ferryman's dwelling overlooking a mile-wide estuary, an artist's studio with a view across a river to woodlands in Cornwall, a remote lodge on the shore of a Scottish loch: I describe my relationship with these, and other, special places.

We can all enjoy the natural world, and we don't necessarily have to go into remote wilderness to find it. My love of 'wildness', my wish to get close in to the life of a place, means I have quite a particular way of doing solitary retreats, a particular emphasis. I am also a Buddhist and so obviously, for me, Buddhist perspectives and practices are intrinsic to the way I approach solitary retreats. However, I have written this book without resorting much to Buddhist terminology, and I trust it will be of interest to anyone drawn to spending time alone in nature. I hope it will inspire other people to undertake solitary retreats and also help them to see how being in nature can be a valuable part of the practice.

There are various ways of doing solitary retreats. This book describes my specific process of discovery, how I found what worked for me. Other people will need to search out the way that works for them. But I am hoping that the story of my journey of exploration will be helpful, even if the route that others take is somewhat different. After the main chapters of the book, which are more descriptive, there is also an appendix with an 'A-to-Z guide' containing practical advice and suggestions for different approaches to solitary retreats.

1

The gaze of the sea

The caravan was in the corner of a field in which sheep grazed, up on a hill looking out to sea on the Llŷn Peninsula in Wales. There was no electricity or running water. But there was a good stock of candles, you could collect water from a nearby stream, and there were also orange bottles of gas to fuel a little cooker and a gas fire.

A friend had generously given me a lift there in his car, and he came in briefly to see the place and have a cup of tea. But then he left me. I was on my own. The caravan seemed suddenly quiet and empty. With a feeling part-way between thrill and shock, it sunk in more fully that I was going to be spending the next fortnight solely in my own company. I realized, with a mixture of excitement and trepidation, that this was the first time in my life I had been utterly alone. Although I was in my early twenties, I had never been completely by myself for two days before, let alone two whole weeks. What I felt in that moment reminded me of what I felt on the day I left home – the day my father had taken me to university for the first term, helped me unload my possessions, said goodbye, and then driven off again, leaving me to fend for myself. There was a similar feeling of growing up, of freedom but also responsibility, of being forced to rely on my own resources.

The landscape was dramatic. Mountains rose sharply and steeply out of the sea: solid, towering, dark verticals, jagged and rugged, directing my gaze upwards, and hinting at challenge and adventure. The sea, in contrast, was open, expansive, spreading, unfolding; it led the eye outwards, beyond the horizon, and suggested a journey, a crossing, an embarking. (I imagined myself to be looking out west into the vast Atlantic, though I realized later that it was, in fact, the Irish Sea.)

After unpacking my few belongings, I walked eagerly down the hill to the coastline. The footpath was steep and passed through a ramshackle and run-down farmyard. It looked like a hard place to make a living. It was a tumbledown farm, only just clinging on, almost at the point of slipping and sliding down the hill. A tangle of barbed wire sagged between half-rotted fence posts so that it was hard to tell if the posts held up the wire, or the wire was holding up the posts. Mud, dilapidated buildings, piles of old tractor tyres, black plastic flapping in the stiff breeze, sorry-looking sheep, wind-slanted gorse, wind-stunted ash: the farm barely hung on; it peered right over the edge into the sea.

Even though it was over twenty-five years ago, I can still clearly remember crossing a field to get to the shore, and there being a double rainbow in front of me. Then a stoat crossed my path just a few yards ahead: utterly alert, sniffing ferociously, its eyes two black diamonds, sharp as scalpels. The way it was wired was so alive and vital. Seeing me, it switched instantly, lashed back on itself, curled like ribbon back into the undergrowth. Its nervous system was strung taut, wound tight, and, at the same time, so supple and sinuous.

Later on that first day, from a certain point along the lane from my caravan, I watched a huge ruby sun set into the sea. I decided I would go back there and watch the sun setting each evening. It would be a way of marking the passing of the days.

What did I intend doing with those days? Mostly nothing. The idea was to step back from the helter-skelter of my life for a while, to step out of my usual routines and habits. I was on retreat in

4

order to get a different perspective on the life I had temporarily left behind.

I had started exploring Buddhism a year or so earlier, and had learnt to meditate, which had been quietly revolutionary. I got to know a whole new person I had never really met before – me. I learnt more about my mind through a few months' meditation than I had learnt in three years at university studying psychology. It was a revelation to begin to understand the thoughts and stories, interpretations and emotional responses that I – consciously and deliberately, or subconsciously and automatically – was choosing every day, and then to see the effect these had on me. Meditation was realizing that you had been trudging round the same old, well-worn streets all your life, lost down dark, narrow alleyways for years, when you could be dancing on the rooftops. Meditation was a bid for freedom.

After a while I had wanted to go on a retreat to learn more and to deepen my experience and practice of meditation, but I didn't have much money. I had heard of some Buddhists doing what they called 'solitaries' – which meant going somewhere quiet and undisturbed for a time to do a retreat on their own. For my first retreat it would perhaps have been more advisable to be part of a supportive group and receive more teaching. However, I knew somewhere I could stay that would be much cheaper than going on an organized group retreat where you would have to pay for the accommodation and catering, as well as the instruction. I knew of this caravan in Wales, which, if my memory serves me correctly, I was able to hire for two pounds per night. Even in those days, a quarter of a century ago, that was very cheap. It meant I could be there for two weeks and feed myself, all for less than fifty pounds.

Money might have been the main reason I gave myself for choosing a solitary retreat, but I suspect there were other motives at play. Being alone appealed to my rather introverted nature, and also I think I was instinctively drawn to being in a wild and open space by myself, with the time to really explore and get to know it. Some of my happiest memories from my childhood and teenage years were of beachcombing rocky coastlines on summer holidays, wandering the woods near where I lived, or tramping the fells of the Lake District with a school friend. Intuitively I knew I wanted to dive deeper into the wildness that I had glimpsed in those places.

A couple of days later I climbed up the nearest hillside, scrambling over rocks and scree. From the top I could see the massive peninsula jutting out westwards, the sea on both sides, and, to the north, the Snowdon range of mountains and the island of Anglesey. It was very quiet; I hadn't met a single person and hadn't spoken a word to anyone for over two days now. There was a build-up of energy inside me – the energy that would usually have been taken up in everyday chatter and in processing the endless stream of sensory input and information that is modern life. That energy wanted an outlet. I had an urge to shout and scream, to make some noise, to hear my own voice speaking out loud. It was also as if, in that silence, I wanted to check if I could still form words and know their meaning. It was almost as though I needed to reassure myself that I wouldn't disappear into the silence. The inner voice of my own thoughts, however, babbled away as usual. It hadn't quietened down much, at least not yet. If anything, being surrounded by silence made that familiar voice and its running commentary sound louder and closer inside my head.

There was a dip on the hilltop and this hollow, combined with the steepness of the hillside, gave the place a distinctive atmosphere. It felt aloft, apart, totally isolated. I had the feeling of being hidden away where no human had ever been before. Just as I was thinking this, and getting into a kind of fantasy about this being my very own secret location, I saw some writing daubed in white paint on a boulder: YOU ENGLISH ARE WELCOME TO VISIT WALES, BUT PLEASE DON'T COME AND LIVE HERE.[2] It made me laugh at myself and at my fantasy of separateness.

I spent those two weeks wandering and exploring, also meditating, reading, and reflecting, or just sitting with a cup of tea in the doorway of my caravan looking out at the view. Whilst in the thick of it, close up, life could seem chaotic and frenetic, as if Jackson Pollock was working overtime right inside my head. But, with the benefit of space and distance, I started to see more patterns and meaning amid the tangle. I was looking for a fresh sense of what I really wanted to be doing with my life, how I wanted to be, what I wanted to give. I wanted to come alive more fully, to taste how *alive* life really could be. Being alone could help me begin to see the wood for the trees, help to strip away the extraneous matter and get to the juicy, sappy essence of what life was really about.

During that fortnight came a torrent of memories from the past. They came welling up in deep dreams, or in streams of images bubbling up in meditation, or in waves of memories washing over me as I sat watching the sea. This process of remembering was spontaneous and unbidden. When I looked back, I realized that the whole flow of memories had occurred in roughly chronological order and that they formed a kind of 'review', a recollecting and reabsorbing, of my life thus far. This has never happened to me in the same way since, though I have known a couple of other people who've had a similar experience.

Sometimes I encountered loneliness, sometimes I felt happy. One minute I would be craving, the next moment I found contentment. Fidgety, restless boredom, then a surprising stillness, sadness, then joy: through being on my own I could see much more clearly how my moment-by-moment experience, the ups and downs of mood, the ever-changing weather patterns of feeling and emotion, arose out of my own mind.

The particular value of a solitary retreat was, of course, the solitude. It threw me back on myself in a particularly strong, uncompromising and valuable way. There was just me, and my thoughts and emotions, my habitual ways of perceiving and thinking. I experienced myself neat, undiluted. I marinated in my own juices. I started to realize how much of my experience – things that I usually attributed to what was going on in the world around me – was, at least to some extent, an interpretation, a mental commentary, a story scribbled by the Jackson Pollock in my own head. But here and now there was no one and nothing else to which to attribute and explain my frame of mind. If I felt irritable I couldn't find fault with an untidy housemate. If I felt anxious I couldn't pin that onto tension amongst colleagues at work. I couldn't blame anyone else; I had to accept responsibility for my moods, for what I had made in my own mind. Through being more aware of those thoughts and emotions, however, there was a kind of confidence, which was liberating and freeing. It meant I could learn to think differently. I had a choice in the matter.

Those two weeks changed me. I became markedly more self-assured and self-reliant. As I wrote in my journal at the time: 'I can survive on my own – more than survive. I can be *me*. I am less afraid of myself.' Looking back twenty-five years later, I find that wording interesting. Maybe we do often live afraid of ourselves, fearful of being ourselves, scared of who we might meet if we spent time alone, frightened of what might happen when left entirely to our own devices. Maybe we worry we will go mad, or implode, or just not cope. I was doing my retreat in the days before mobile-phone and internet communication. Nowadays we are even less likely to be truly alone for more than a few minutes, and perhaps for many people the thought of solitude can seem even more frightening. However, I also know from conversations with other people who've spent time like this, on their own, that the first feelings of anxiety can soon give way to a new-found freedom and joy. Yes, we will have our ups and downs, but we will also discover sources of confidence and happiness that we hardly knew existed.

The gaze of the sea

At the end of the fortnight I walked back down the hill to the main road and hitched a lift to Bangor and the nearest train station. I didn't have to wait long for a lift. The second car that came along slowed and then stopped, and two friendly Welsh women – a mother and her daughter – picked me up. In the car they taught me how to say 'I've been to Wales' in Welsh and we laughed at my attempts at pronunciation. They enquired about what I'd been doing. I said I'd been walking up in the hills for a couple of weeks. Then they asked where my friends were. When I said I'd been on my own they were surprised, to say the least, and I think they even felt a bit sorry for me.

But I was happy. It had been a life-changing two weeks. I was returning home palpably different, more grounded and self-aware. I sat on the train amongst the mums trying to soothe discontented babies and overexcited school kids running up and down the carriage shouting and laughing. Usually I might have got a bit irritated at all the noise, but right then I felt buoyant and stable, as though something of the open ocean and the unshakeable mountains had stayed with me. I felt happy just to be myself, and, simultaneously, 'protected' – as though nothing could touch me, as if I was wrapped in a force field of light. The experience didn't last, of course, but it was still valuable; it taught me something about the power and potential of time alone.

Up in that caravan on the Llŷn Peninsula I had learnt the value of solitude. The way I was reflected back to myself, being confronted with my essential aloneness, had not, after all, been too challenging and frightening, but freeing and enriching. Through finding out that I could happily be alone *with* myself I discovered that I was happy to *be* myself. That might not sound like much of a revelation, but I had found a level of self-esteem and self-ease that, though basic, is essential. It was the beginning of a practice of solitude and of solitary retreats that I have continued through my life.

Almost every year since then I have gone away on my own for a while, for a month if time has allowed, or a couple of weeks, or for however long I have been able to manage. I have been doing this nearly every year for over twenty-five years now. I go somewhere quiet and close to nature. I try and find a place to stay that is simple, basic, uncluttered. I keep it as free as possible from distraction. I take no computer. I switch off my mobile phone. I don't want a place that comes with a television or an internet connection. I want to spend that time completely alone.

Learning about the value of solitude wasn't the only realization I had up on that Welsh hillside. I also discovered, or rediscovered, the value of wild places and the importance of those places in our inner journeys. For what had happened to me there was partly a product of the mountains and the sea. The wildness of the place helped unleash the wildness of my mind. There were thoughts, feelings, and reflections that came to me because of those rocky summits with the huge sky above, or that came whilst I watched the red sun melting into the sea.

On the last night of my time there, as had been my little daily ritual, I had been to watch the sunset. It was such a calm evening that the sea, from where I was up on the hill, appeared totally still. So still, in fact, that it didn't look like the sea, or at all watery, but like a great expanse of purple-blue ice, which reflected and refracted the colours of the sky. They were colours from some unmapped zone of the spectrum, colours from way over the horizon, colours beyond words, ungraspable, secret and mysterious, like those on the lustrous inner surface of a seashell. Where the light of the setting sun was reflected was like a pathway across the ice. And I suddenly felt as though someone – a friend, or perhaps even myself – was making their way along that pathway, stepping out across that expanse of ice and sea, embarking on a long voyage towards the fire of the sun. It wasn't that I actually saw a vision in front of me. It was more an inner sense, but one that was so intense and definite that it seemed as if I really was watching a journey commence in front of me. It came with a strange mixture of sadness and joy: sadness as if at a parting, but also relief and happiness in knowing that the journey had begun.

My stay on the Llŷn Peninsula was the first time I'd been really alone, but as a child I had always hankered after wild and beautiful places. On family holidays by the seaside my brother and I would, like many children, go exploring rock pools. In my memory we ran full speed, skipping across the rocks, leaping barefoot from one rock to another, never missing our footing. Maybe my memory is exaggerating the naturalness with which we made our way over the sharp and slippery stone, but I am sure we were, compared to my adult self, quick and agile. We wanted to get to the largest and deepest pools, and we would go further out and further round the shore, beyond the crowds, to find them.

There they would be: secret sea-gardens, lush with seaweeds, tangled with emerald, draped with gold, filigreed with delicate and intricate lacework of coral red. There was a whole world of fascination beneath our feet. For that world to emerge fully, for all its secrets to be revealed, we had to make ourselves quiet and still. Gradually fishes appeared out of nowhere, crabs shuffled out from underneath the seaweed, semi-transparent shrimps swam into full view. A shell lying on a rock wobbled slightly and then upended itself and a creature – a hermit crab – emerged. From an amber blob of jelly, tentacles unfurled and groped around – a sea anemone. If we looked even more carefully then shells and limpets could be seen to be cautiously shifting position. In one pool I saw sliding across the bottom what looked in size and shape like a foot, but with appendages that waved in the watery depths. It sent a shudder up my spine; I didn't know what it could possibly be. Years later I discovered that probably it was a sea slug.

To really see what was there, my brother and I had to pretend not to be there. Just a jolt from either of us and the fish would bolt back into the dark crevices, gone in an instant, like lightning flashes. I was later to discover that meditation is something like gazing into a rock pool. We have to quietly sit and watch. We can't hurry the process or make happen what we want to happen. We have to learn stillness and a less obvious, more subtle, way of 'doing' meditation. If we are still enough, then gradually, out of the depths, creatures – deeper thoughts and emotions – will shyly emerge. But try to make a grab for them and they dash back into the darkness.

During art classes at school I once painted a picture of a young woman standing on a rocky shoreline, her hair blowing in the wind, looking out to sea. In the distance there was an old sailing boat and you couldn't quite tell if this ship was sailing into land or away from it, whether it was coming home or departing. The art teacher, Mrs Lovegrove, had a good way with teenagers; she knew how to win their trust and encourage them. She suggested that I might be painting myself. The figure I had painted was a woman, so it wasn't me in a literal sense, but rather more symbolically.

I think she was right. The painting was maybe rather dreamy and innocent, but I was – quite unconsciously – putting into paint what I was feeling at the time. The figure was looking out to sea longingly, looking for something, a bit lost and unsure. During family holidays in the summer vacation I loved to go off by myself to some quiet spot where I could gaze at the sea. The sea's endless changing absorbed me; it soaked up all my attention. Without quite knowing it myself – certainly without being able to explain it to others – I was looking out to that distant horizon, waiting, longing, wondering what might lie beyond. All this had, without me being aware of it, found its way into my painting.

It was a time in my life when I could see no sense or meaning. To me back then it seemed that life stretched on rather dismally for a few decades, came to a sudden stop, and beyond this horizon I could see nothing. It seemed incredible that we were now so alive, but that this life would one day be taken from us. This really appalled me and made everything seem pointless and futile. I couldn't understand how my contemporaries just carried on as if nothing was the matter. How could people remain satisfied with ordinary, mundane things? It wasn't that I was depressed; I always had plenty of energy and interest in things. But, on their own, they just weren't enough. I longed for deeper meaning and purpose.

Then, at eighteen years of age, I went to university in one of the UK's big cities. I remember on the very first evening a group of us were sitting round the kitchen table in our accommodation block talking. In turn each person said what course they were doing, what job this would lead to, and, most importantly, what they expected to earn once they graduated. I said nothing; for me it was a moment of heart-sinking disillusionment. Looking back now, from a longer perspective, I see that we were 'Thatcher's children' – a product of the 1980s with its mass unemployment and the emerging culture of harder-edged materialism and individualism. Many of us were the first members of our respective families to go to university and we had gone there in order to get good jobs, not so much in order to get a 'good education'. Despite the conventional image of students as radicals, many of my generation were conservative and career orientated. I felt like an outsider politically and I had no idea what career I wanted to pursue. Though I did eventually make friends and find people I had more in common with, I never felt that I fitted in or that I really belonged there.

I was an ordinary boy from the leafy suburbs transplanted into the middle of a metropolis. Six lanes of traffic rumbled along the expressway immediately outside the tower block in which I lived. It was a shock; I felt out of place. Maybe it had all been a horrible mistake.

I discovered that behind the back streets were miles of old canals, surrounded by disused and abandoned factories and industrial buildings. Strewn along the towpaths were old shopping trollies, used condoms, a burnt motorcycle tyre, a set of National Health Service crutches, and colour-faded crisp packets. In those days hardly anyone went there – just the occasional jogger, or a student taking a shortcut – and once I had turned a corner under a bridge and almost walked into an adolescent boy sniffing glue.

One day along the canal I saw an old man in a big black overcoat. He was pushing a wheelbarrow, but then he stopped, bent over the side of the water and pulled something out on a rope. It looked like a bag, a bloated bag made of sacking. He put it in his wheelbarrow and moved on another ten yards and then did the same thing again. I had no idea what he was doing, but it looked strange, even sinister, and I didn't want to go near, let alone ask him what was going on. For some reason it put me in mind of a scene from Dickens: I felt like Pip on the eerie Kent Marshes, witnessing something that he was not meant to have seen. It remained a mystery to me for several years, until someone told me the man was probably pulling up traps he'd laid for eels.

It wasn't exactly a natural environment, but it wasn't quite man-made either. It was more like a post-human world that nature was taking back. A white swan swam on the oil-black water. A pied wagtail hurried along the towpath. Ivy and bindweed clambered over the rust-red corrugated iron fence. Rosebay willowherb sent spikes of pink fire spurting out of chinks in the brickwork. A kestrel flickered up onto the roof of a cavernous warehouse. A full-sized buddleia grew out of the tiniest crack in the concrete, sending its sweet scent into the air.

Many of these canal ways have since been redeveloped. Humans have taken them back again, converted the old warehouses into flats and penthouses, opened up cafés and restaurants on the waterfronts, transformed the towpaths into byways for bustling tourists. But for me back then, though they were hardly the leafy woodlands of my childhood, those places were a world, a terrain, that I found intriguing, strangely and surprisingly enchanting. I couldn't even quite say I enjoyed it, but I found something I needed there. It was a space, a clearing, in which I could find myself.

A few years later I looked out to sea on the last night of my time on the Llŷn Peninsula. I saw the light of the setting sun form a pathway across the water and, quite clearly and definitely, I had the sense of someone stepping out along that pathway, starting out on a journey towards that sun. And I knew that I had come to a significant juncture in my life. After the uncertainty of my teenage years, after my disorientating time at university, during which I had no idea what I was going to do with my life, I could at last see in a new direction. I had made some good friends at university, but I could tell that our ways in life were, perhaps inevitably, diverging. I was sad about that, but there was also relief that I had found a pathway, and I was beginning a new journey.

The gazing out to sea *helped* me to that realization. Its mood and motion, the way the sea unfolded and stretched to the horizon, shaped and expanded my inner world. The landscape, the interplay between the bold mountains and the open sea, contributed to the weight and significance of what I discovered. Something of my inner landscape was mirrored in the outer landscape, so I could see it more clearly. Something of that outer landscape reflected back again, casting new light on the inner. There was a reciprocity in which the usual boundary between inner and outer, or subject and object, became more diaphanous, less fixed and definite.

That land had a power to shape and colour how I thought and felt. The form and texture of that landscape formed and textured my imagination. I wouldn't have expressed it to myself like that back then, but now I see how the more alert and attentive we are, the more the world will come alive, speaking or gesturing to us in particular ways. We need images and metaphors with which to think and feel. The wild is full of images and metaphors, and so has a particular power to influence our thinking and feeling. Consciously or unconsciously, we weave threads and fabrics from the wild world into the warp and weft that is our interpreting and imagining. That is partly what poets and artists are doing, paying conscious attention to the correspondence of 'inner' and 'outer' experience, being open and alive to the possibility of resonance.

Psychologists have researched the beneficial effects of natural environments on the development of children's imagination. Children love to play in green spaces because they give more scope for imagination and fantasy than a plainer, concrete playground. Natural places are more 'open-ended', more animated and alive, more suggestive; they have more to say. They are more play-full! No doubt all this holds true for adults too. The ever-changing variety of nature, the fact that it has no immediate utilitarian value, the way that it engages all the senses without grabbing at them, can, if we allow it, help drop us down into a deeper, more poetic and metaphorical way of being with the world.

Places, perhaps especially wild places, can talk to us; they can be full of suggestion and meaning. Inner and outer worlds can mirror each other, and this changes our awareness. Maybe it is easier for children to see the world animated in this way. Perhaps this way of relating to the world also comes more naturally to people in premodern cultures. To them, the world is alive, and the particular energy and atmosphere of a place might be experienced as a deity – such as a tree spirit, or a water nymph – a *genius loci*, a spirit of the place. For us, with our scientific materialist upbringing, such a mode of perception may not come so naturally. But nor does the world need to be entirely dead and inert, deaf and dumb, to us. We can find our way back; we can learn to listen with care and attentiveness, we can learn to talk with the world again. If we're aware and awake enough, the wild will speak with us.

2

The secret valley

Not far from the Spanish Mediterranean coast, not so many miles inland from the beaches, clubs, and bars of Benidorm, and the sun seeking, fun chasing, holiday making of the Costa del Sol, lies the Sierra Aitana range of mountains. Some way up one of the few windy, rough, and rutted dirt tracks that run through this wild and lesser-known region of Spain, there is, hidden away in a valley, a Buddhist retreat centre known as 'Guhyaloka', which means 'the secret, mysterious realm'. It may not be many miles away from the Mediterranean coast, but it is another world entirely.

Steep and high cliffs made of limestone flank the valley, seeming to seal off and enclose, to guard and offer protection. The rock is blue-grey and bleached-bone white, with seams of sandy orange. On top of the cliffs, stones and boulders are scattered about, their distinctive convex and concave shapes like the remains of old skulls, bones, and bone sockets. From up here, looking out from the valley, there are a series of higher ridges curving like ancient, semi-derelict boundary walls; the jagged tops are like the crenellations of once-great fortresses.

There is something almost brittle and metallic in the feel of the rock, but it is hard and tough, and it gives a good grip to your boots. It is made, of course, from remains of sea creatures deposited on the ocean bed millions of years ago, and, over time, compressed into rock. Then, through the collision of continents, the opposing trajectory of tectonic plates, the beds of rock were turned vertical and thrust upwards, creating these spectacular ridges and dramatic cliffs. They say that the higher the mountain is, the bigger the collision that led to its formation, and, therefore, the more deep down and ancient the strata of rock that it arose from. The high ridges were once part of an ocean bed; the sheer cliffs are the result of colossal geological forces acting over vast spans of time.

In the valley itself, as in many of the surrounding valleys and hillsides, almonds and olives were once grown and harvested. Going back to Moorish times, huge areas of forest were cleared and terraced with drystone walls. Olive trees were planted and, later, almond trees. Other crops were cultivated underneath the trees, as well as pasture for goats and sheep to graze. But, in the twentieth century, as world markets opened up, the almond groves ceased to be profitable and most of them were abandoned. What would have once been thriving and busy areas of agricultural activity have become wild and unpopulated again. The terraces are gradually crumbling, the trees are now old and unkempt. Underneath the trees meadow flowers and sun-bleached grasses are gradually being outgrown by shrubs and thorny bushes. They, in their turn, are slowly overtaken by pine trees and holm oak. The valleys are filling out with a deeper green; the forest is returning.

Though no longer tended, the almond trees blossom very early in the spring, and there is still a crop of nuts, and also of olives. The trees are like dancing skeletons, twisting and waving their knees and knuckles, their elbows and bones. Some of the olive trees in the region are very old indeed, even dating back hundreds of years to the end of the Moorish period, and there is now a market for uprooting them from their native soil, exporting them, and selling them in garden centres for a hefty profit.

There are large areas where the pine woodland is now well established, with the much slower-growing holm oak finding its footing beneath the taller pine trees, or on the edge of the woods, or on the stones and scree sloping up to the cliffs. Underneath the pines rosemary and juniper, thyme and rock rose also grow. It is a place where only the spiky and spiny, the wizened and wiry, the hard-edged and wax-leaved shrubs and plants can live. These are the ones that can survive the harsh elements, the snow and cold of winter, and then the baking sun and drying wind of summer.

In springtime and early summer nightingales sing. Choughs wheel about the cliffs, nesting in the many gaps and crevices. They call repeatedly at each other, *cheow-cheow-cheow*, and the noise rebounds off the valley walls, like the ricocheting of bullets in a spaghetti western. There are big alpine swifts that fly fearsomely close over the heads of anyone standing on the cliff tops. There are birds of prey: falcons dashing, eagles ranging, vultures mooching. At home I have a large black vulture's feather given to me by an old friend. The man who gave it to him was watching a vulture fly across the valley one day. It suddenly stopped flapping its wings, came to a halt in mid-air, and plummeted out of the sky. It died just like that, whilst flying. It quite literally dropped dead. He managed to find the bird and took a few of its feathers.

The heady, warm, and woody aroma of pine resin hits the back of the nostrils in the hot of summer. Silence, and then a sudden, sharp crack as a pine cone expands and opens out in the heat. Sometimes there is a great roar of wind rising up the valley, like a huge rushing wave, flooding the trees with sound. It comes rolling upwards, surging through the woodland, and often you hear the noise in the distance long before you feel the warm air against your skin. There are snakes and iridescent lizards, gorgeous butterflies and flowers, scorpions and big spiders, wild boar, and, sometimes, wild cats and deer up on the hilltops. The whole valley is alive.

This is a particularly special place for many people, as each year there is a four-month retreat in which a group of men are ordained into the Triratna Buddhist Order. (The ordination of women takes place at another retreat centre further north in Spain.) That was how I first found myself in the 'secret valley'; I was on such a retreat here with sixteen other men in the mid-1990s. My interest in Buddhism had consolidated to the point of wanting to be ordained and become part of an Order, or community, of like-minded practitioners. The ordination didn't necessitate having to adopt a particular lifestyle; it wasn't monastic, nor was it lay. It was about fully dedicating myself to following the Buddha, to putting his teaching – the principles and practices that Buddhists call the 'Dharma' – at the centre of my life, and trying to express these values as fully as possible in my friendships, relationships, work, and in all the activities of my life.

Finding the Dharma was like finding a map that made sense and by which I could orientate myself. My life now had direction and purpose. This was a profound relief after the earlier period at school and university when I felt rather lost and dislocated. So I was throwing in my lot with the Buddha; I was gladly and willingly going to travel his way. I also felt a sense of gratitude towards the Buddhists who had helped get me this far and I wanted to try and give something back.

So all seventeen of us on that retreat left behind our ordinary lives, homes, careers, and relationships, and made the journey to this special place. Underneath those tall cliff walls we did feel guarded and protected, safe from the outside world. The valley in between those towering cliff faces also seemed like a container, a crucible, a place of fiery transformation. Guhyaloka lived up to its name; it was hidden away, secret, even mysterious and mythical; it was where we found out who we really were, what we were capable of becoming.

During the retreat we would sometimes all climb up onto the cliffs so that, in effect, we formed a circle and faced each other across the valley walls. We would chant mantras as loud as we could and listen to them echoing and re-echoing back and forth. Towards the end of the retreat something else happened. It was dusk, and there had been a heavy rainstorm. Part of the sky was still black-blue, but the sun was also breaking back through. It was one of those half-dark, half-light skies: a sky cut clean in two. The rock faces glowed gold in the dying sunlight. One last time we went up on top of the ridges, but this time we faced outwards. The twinkling lights of towns and villages were starting to emerge in the distance. Each of us read favourite texts, poems, and inspirational verses out towards the world. We were doing this to signify that we were shortly going back to the world, and we wanted to take something back with us. We wanted to have something new to give once we returned to our familiar lives. We had come away to this special place, but we had come in order to go back home again.

Shortly after my return to the UK I started working at my local Buddhist centre – a very direct and obvious way to try and give something back. In time, we opened much bigger premises and I became director of the new centre, organizing activities, teaching many of the classes, and generally overseeing the whole project. We started several satellite groups in neighbouring towns and cities. I was now in my early thirties. This period was, for me, highly engaged and directed, heady, energized. I was intensely idealistic, probably at times rather earnest, and very ambitious. It was the phase of my life that burnt, burnt like a blowtorch, burnt with a pure, bright flame.

It wasn't just a job; it was a whole way of life. My days were spent working at the Buddhist Centre, my evenings teaching Buddhist classes, and I returned home at night to the Buddhist community where I lived. I ate, drank, and breathed Buddhism. It was my work and my play, my night and my day. It was a way of life that required 'going out' strongly: meeting lots of people, communicating from the heart, being to some extent a 'public' figure. But I also had a strongly introverted temperament, a quieter side. I learnt, sometimes the painful way – by getting almost burnt out – that if all this 'going out' was to be sustainable then I needed to 'go in' strongly too. The 'going in' could be reinvigorating, and enabled me to 'go out' again. The 'going out' drew forth, tested and then consolidated what I had discovered through 'going in'. Sometimes it was necessary to get away and be a 'hermit'; other times I was the 'activist'. I needed to give enough time and space to both modes, both ways of being. At its best, there was a balance and a reciprocal relationship between the two.

And so I returned to Guhyaloka a number of times in the next years to do solitary retreats. There were a number of secluded spots, away from the main centre, where I could stay. I would sometimes arrive rather exhausted, overfull and overdone, and longing to be by myself for a while. I was relieved to have escaped that busy life; I could hardly wait to be alone. But after settling in for a few days, all by myself in that remote mountainous valley, I would start thinking and reflecting on the life I'd left behind. That world back home would be very much on my mind and in my meditations. After a couple of weeks, inspiration would suddenly arise again in my meditation, or whilst I walked the cliff tops. I would return home recharged, pumped up and full of bounce, eager to get back to the project, keen to try out new ideas. I left that busy world behind, and returned uplifted and inspired, with a fresh perspective. I left, but I left in order to go back home again. I retreated, re-formed, and then re-engaged more strongly. There was a rhythm to my life that, for a while at least, really worked for me. The solitary retreats of those years were a crucial ingredient in an inspired and creative chapter of my life. I loved coming to this place and, for a while, being able to 'face in' – into this secret valley and into myself – so that eventually I was ready to 'face out' to the world again.

My favourite place to stay was a very basic wooden hut, built by the friend who had given me the vulture's feather during the time he lived here in the valley. I loved the spot the hut was in, down near the bottom of the valley, quite close under a huge, sheer cliff, nearly 200 metres high, that was known as 'the whale'. Looking up at the face of the rock, I would watch the forms and colours shift through the day as the sun changed position. In the early morning it could be a rosy pink, by midday it might be grey and hazy in the heat, as the sun descended westwards it became pitted and pockmarked with stark shadows, and then gradually it would turn gold.

The hut was roughly built, but I liked it. There was a platform outside which I sometimes used for meditating. Occasionally, when I opened my eyes, a gecko was climbing up a tree trunk inches from my head or a snake was easing quietly through the undergrowth. If it sensed my presence, however, the snake cracked like a whip, and writhed away in an instant. During the night there could be disconcerting thumps and scratches behind the walls or under the floor of the cabin. But I grew to feel quite safe and happy there.

The 'kitchen' was an old, no longer roadworthy VW van, parked a little way from the hut, and kitted out with a gas ring, basic supplies, and utensils. After a while I noticed that some little creature was chewing the top of my plastic bottle of sunflower oil. I stacked up a few tins and jars, and placed the bottle of oil on top of them where I thought the creature wouldn't be able to reach it.

The next day I was cooking and reached to pour some oil into a wok. I picked up the bottle, began to pour, and then nearly dropped it. There was something moving inside. Somehow a mouse had climbed the tins and jars, up the side of the bottle, gnawed through the plastic top, and then fallen into the oil. It must have been desperate. It was lucky that there were only a couple of inches of oil left in the bottle; if there had been more it would have drowned. I took it outside and carefully tipped the bottle up, pouring the oil away and allowing the mouse to get out to safety. It was drenched in sunflower oil, its fur matted and bedraggled, and it moved away slowly and sorrowfully, or so it seemed to me. But at least it hadn't been stir-fried.

Once I climbed up to the steep-sided ridge on one side of the valley. The ridge ran east–west and I went up to it from the northern side. Here, just under the ridge, it was surprisingly cold. No sun ever shone there – it was always in shadow. The flora was totally strange and unfamiliar, foreign, like I had somehow walked straight into another country with a different climate. Plants with clusters of white flowers on long stalks, with fleshy, succulent, grey-green leaves, grew straight out of the rock. But once on the top I was in the more familiar Mediterranean environment, with its sharp-edged grey limestone, and the spiky plants that evolved to withstand the harsh heat and the drying wind, amongst which large, bright butterflies swirled about. Occasionally an inch-long creature would hover up to the flowers, wings whirring, and unfurl a delicate filament into the flower to 'drink' the nectar – a hummingbird moth.

I walked along the ridge, admiring the fantastic view and the sparkling blue Mediterranean in the distance. My plan was to follow the ridge along, come down the other side and then walk back up the valley to where I was staying. I could see how and where the ridge curved its way, like the vertebrae of a spine, and I had been told there was a path down at the other end. The ridge got narrower and narrower till eventually there was a sheer drop on either side. It became less like walking and more like climbing and clambering. The beginnings of fear started lurking deep in my being, but I hoped it would be alright if I kept going.

Then, suddenly, there was no ridge. It just fell away in front of me, as well as to left and right. There was a chunk missing. It was only a chunk; a few yards beyond this the ridge carried on as before. But where I now stood there were sheer verticals on three sides of me. I wondered if I could climb down and across the gap and then continue along the ridge as I'd wanted. I'm a pretty good climber and I thought I had a reasonably good head for heights. But welling up in me was a gut instinct to try no such thing.

I was alone up there, miles from anyone, and no one knew where I was. If I fell, the long fall to the rocks below would almost certainly kill me. If I got stuck, there would have been no way I could call for help. And then, what had begun as a feeling of caution suddenly escalated. Starting low in the lurching stomach, clawing its way up into the thudding heart, creeping all over my juddering body, triggering my thinking mind into overdrive: panic, panic, panic, panic. I watched thoughts invading my being like alien intruders: 'I can't do this, I'm stuck. I can't do this, I'm stuck.' For a few moments I was going mad; though I could see what was going on in my mind, I could not control it. As well as being cognitive, it was also emotional and absolutely visceral. It required all my mental effort to prevent the panic from taking me over and paralyzing me. I had to work hard to keep my head, to keep the thoughts of freezing terror under control, and to tell myself to slowly turn my shaking body around, to hold onto those rocks with my fumbling hands, and to scramble back. It wasn't till I had retreated quite a way, to where the ridge widened out once more, that I began to relax, breathe more easily, and feel safe again.

On another retreat I learnt more about how such missing chunks in a ridge came about. I was staying in a stone-built dwelling further up the valley, during the wettest autumn the locals had known for many years. There had been days and days of drumming rain. In Britain all that rain would have turned quickly into streams and waterfalls across the hillside. Water would be gushing through every gash in the rock, converting stony pathways into streams. The far mountainside would be streaked with new seams of silver, the waterfalls frothing and furious, the air saturated with the voices of water: whispering, then chattering, then roaring. The stepping stones would be submerged in a rush of tea-brown, the grassy paths sodden and pulped to mud, the bracken flood-flattened, the bog unpassable, the rain-filled air getting the cold and wet everywhere, in the eyes, ears, face, clothes, and boots.

But here in this mountain valley it had rained for days and there were no rivers or streams anywhere. It had been so dry for months beforehand that the earth was like a great sponge that could soak up whatever the sky threw down. It was true that the dust-orange tracks had turned to sticky mud that clung in great gluey clods to my boots and made every footstep heavy, as if someone had turned up the gravity dial of the planet. There were even a few milky-orange puddles. But otherwise more and more water fell to the ground, which just absorbed and contained it. The summer-baked soil stored it up and hid it away, or else the rain disappeared into the cracks and grykes between the lumps of limestone.

All that water seemed to just vanish. But there was more going on than the eye could see. All along the cliff top it trickled into crevices and fault lines in the rock. Drip by drip it washed away the last pockets of clay and debris from around boulders. It was soaked up by thirsty roots of trees, which grew and swelled and opened up the fault lines a fraction further.

Until, one night, at a particular point on that huge rock face, the massive weight of one boulder no longer had enough support underneath it. With a fearsome crack it suddenly gave way, and the boulder, several tons of it, went hurtling into empty space.

I was sitting in my cabin in the dark, with my eyes closed, quietly meditating, at the moment it happened. I heard the crack, then silence, then a crashing sound, smashing, sliding, and scraping. I had no idea what it could be. My first thought was that a car had slid off the road and had rolled over and down one of the terraces. I raced outside, my heart hammering. But the noise continued and I realized it couldn't be a car. I also realized that, whatever it was, it sounded close and it was getting louder.

Then the noise stopped. There was just ominous silence and complete darkness. Beneath the thick cloud there was no moon, no stars, no light whatsoever, not even any dark shadows or vague inky shapes. The world had disappeared, had been secreted away. There was just absolute nothingness, a void in which I stood all alone. I waved my torch around, wishing desperately I could conjure that vanished world into becoming visible again. In the feeble torchlight a section of tree trunk reappeared, or a slice of a terrace wall, but I could not see much further beyond that. It was useless trying to make out what had happened. I hurried back inside, my heart still banging.

In daylight the next morning I went out again to see if I could discover the reason for all that noise and commotion. Beyond my cabin was a boulder, about two metres wide, that hadn't been there the day before. Beyond it was a series of split branches, smashed stone walls, and huge gashes in the ground. From those track marks I could judge the trajectory of the rock; it looked pretty much in line with my cabin, and had stopped only twenty yards short. I was able to follow the track of the rock further back and I could just make out the point high up on the cliff top from which the boulder had fallen. The trail of destruction caused as it had crashed down the scree slope was clearly visible. Trunks and branches of holm-oak trees were split and splayed out either side of the path the rock had taken. On the road below there wasn't a mark; it must have hit the bottom of the scree slope, bounced, and flown through the air before hitting the ground again several metres away on the other side of the road.

Those rocks and cliffs, formed millions of years ago, might have seemed timeless, impassive, unchanging – yet it was not so. Everything is always changing. The rate of change might vary, but the inevitability of change remains the same. Now I could even more vividly appreciate the secret valley as a place that was vital and elemental, so full of the forces of change, a place animated by both surging growth and dramatic decay.

Just over a year later I lodged in the stone cabin in the early winter. The sun was lower in the sky and showed above the cliff tops for far fewer hours each day. It could still feel warm when the sun was high enough to spill into the valley, but the very moment the sun went below the cliff it became chilly. A few days later it snowed unseasonably early. The snow was sleety, the trunks of the pine trees turned dark chocolate, the air was cold and damp, and the atmosphere, the sound of the whole place, was silenced, shushed, by snow. Soon, however, it melted and there was a constant background sound of dripping and draining as wet snow trickled down tree trunks, or splatters as sopping snow flopped off branches, or bigger splashes as snow slewed off the roof of the cabin.

There was a little wood-burning stove inside, but the chimney was blocked and I couldn't get the stove to draw properly. The room just filled with smoke. I decided to simply do without the fire. I told myself I could cope with the cold. Looking back now I wonder why I didn't get someone to come and fix the stove. I still don't fully understand why, though I think I have an inkling of the reason. I was so absorbed in my retreat that I didn't want to interrupt it and be disturbed. I was young and ardent!

This was also what I now refer to as my 'angry retreat'. I'd arrived with underlying frustration at certain people and events back home, and on the retreat all those seething emotions erupted into full-blown anger and resentment. Back home, the busyness of life, the possibility of distraction, and the wish to be seen in a good light by others could damp down unwelcome emotions to some extent. But here, the solitude, the hours of meditation, and the raw, elemental environment created an opening through which everything came to the surface. It was a safe space in which the volcano could explode. Some days I found myself stomping up and down the pathway outside my hut, while tired old arguments shuttled back and forth inside my head. All I could do was try not to give way to the internal voices of blame and self-pity, try to view the situation from a more helpful perspective, try to have more kindness for myself and the others involved. I knew that I had to work really hard to contain and transform these destructive emotions. If I didn't, if I just let them rip, then my experience would become even more hellish. So I ignored the freezing conditions and the stove that didn't draw. I wanted to stay completely vigilant with regard to my mind, and in some strange way the weather provided a cold, keen edge to the discipline of that.

I wore every item of clothing I had with me, day and night, and wrapped myself in every available blanket, as well as enveloping myself inside my sleeping bag. I realized that I'd have to be alert and not allow the cold to get me into a negative frame of mind. When I went for walks, however, I soon warmed up. In the end I managed surprisingly easily and even strangely relished my ability to survive there, although it is not an experience I would want to repeat! As my time there drew to a close I felt it had been a hard but necessary task, and that it was work well done. I returned home much happier and healthier than I had been on arrival.

On my first solitary retreat, on the Llŷn Peninsula, the towering mountains and the wide-open sea had mirrored my inner life back at me so I could see it more clearly and sense my way forward. Here also, the sheer cliff faces of the secret valley held and contained me, and reflected me back to myself. The landscape was like a friend; the place itself became part of the process and experience of transformation.

3

Mind is more fleet than the feet

It was summer and I was driving north to the highlands of Scotland. The A82 wound its way through steep hills, straightjacketed by monotonous, overcrowded forestry plantations, hemmed in by the uniform lines of identikit spruce trees, shoulder to shoulder in their green-black greatcoats, rigid and expressionless. But then the road went over a hill and entered Glencoe. And at exactly that point a road sign said: 'Welcome to the Highlands.'

I drove over the brow of the hill and I entered another world. The light and the land changed. That day, as I was driving into it, it was a place of luminous skies and tumbling clouds. The world suddenly expanded, became spacious, a vast moorland of rich ochre, with opalescent tarns. To the north, great mountains drew me forward. Did whoever put that sign up do so simply because an official boundary intersects with the road at just that point? Or had they chosen the spot because they also noticed that transformation of the land? I felt I had been ferried over a border, transported into another realm.

Despite crossing over a threshold into a new landscape, I had many miles still to go. I was heading north of Ullapool, almost to the very north-west tip of Scotland, to stay in a wooden shack that was rented out for retreats. The owner, Mrs Hammond, was a lively, spirited lady, with a shock of white hair and steel-blue eyes. The cabin was down on the beach near where she lived, and her children, and then her grandchildren, had used it as a beach hut in years gone by. Mrs Hammond spent the winter in London and the summer months up in her cottage in the Highlands. Some months earlier, when I'd spoken to her on the phone to ask if I could stay in the cabin, she'd said, 'Oh yes dear, of course you can stay there, as long as it is still standing when the spring comes.'

Luckily for me, the winter gales hadn't blown it down and it was still standing. It was a small cabin, with a bunk bed, a porcelain basin for washing, a two-ring cooker and gas bottle, a plastic cooler box for keeping food in, and various other paraphernalia: old blankets, fishing rods, boat oars, children's seaside bucket and spades, a ball of orange nylon string, shells and pebbles. Water came from a stream nearby, and there was a chemical loo in a tent round the back. The cabin was down beyond a lightly wooded hill behind the village where Mrs Hammond lived. It was set back from a tiny little beach, mostly pebbled and rocky, but with patches of sand. Further on from the beach, the coast was rocky, with numerous islets not far offshore. When I got there it was evening time and there was a mist of midges and mosquitoes. But, to me, it was idyllic.

I had been up this far north only once before, on holiday with a friend, had been utterly entranced, and had been waiting for a chance to come back. Now I had that opportunity. I was going to be spending a whole four weeks here. My previous times alone had been for one or usually two weeks. Just once I'd gone for as long as three weeks. This time I felt ready to try a full month. I knew those previous times of solitude had a strong effect on me, and I wanted to see whether, if I stayed for longer, the effect would continue and consolidate. What would a whole month alone be like? Could I sustain this much longer period? Over a week or a fortnight you could easily count how many days remained before it was time to go home again, but a month felt significantly different. Needing to rely entirely on my own inner resources for a whole month was more of a stretch and a challenge.

It was June and that meant the days were light and long. In fact, it hardly got dark at all, merely dusky. At about midnight the sun skimmed just beneath the horizon for barely a couple of hours before slanting upwards again. This virtually simultaneous sunset-sunrise took place to the north. The sun set just a few degrees to the west of north and came up again just a few degrees east of it. It then spent the next twenty-two hours circling the whole huge sky.

In the course of my time there, only one other person came down to the beach, a man who, one fine day, turned up and spent the afternoon fishing. The only other people I saw were on little fishing boats that passed by, with a throaty *putter-putter-putter* of their diesel engines. Sometimes people waved from the boats, and one time I heard a man say to his companion, 'That's the Buddhist retreat you know!'

I loved watching the swinging sea, the slow sway of seaweed, the dash of fish, the awkward sideling clamber of a crab, and gulls with that distinctive bounce in their wingbeat. I spent hours watching fulmars looping the loop; they'd arc round and up to their nesting point on the cliffs and then, at the last moment, decide not to land after all, but arc round one more time, just for the love of it. An otter rummaged on the shoreline, following its nose. Seals poked their heads out of the sea and looked about them. Deer quietly watched me from the hill above. Orchids grew in abundance, purple-pink on the grassy, hummocky roadsides, and there were small lochs where red-throated divers nested. Many of these lochs were thick with water lilies. Black-backed gulls would float over my head, cocking their head in order to look down, calling – *wuck-wuck-wuck* – at me.

There were mountains in the distance, and they had beautiful, evocative names, such as Suilven, Canisp, or Quinag, names derived from the Vikings who were intrigued by these mountains and their magic and majesty. (Sutherland, the name of this region of Scotland, means 'southern lands' and is again Nordic in origin.) Mostly the landscape was open and relatively flat, and the mountains were spaced apart, rising straight up out of the land and sea. This made them appear quite distinctive, and also made them look bigger and higher than they actually were.

A couple of curious things happened. The first was that one day huge numbers of pale-pink jellyfish were washed up on the beach. There were yards and yards of jellyfish strewn everywhere, flopped on the pebbles, seeming lifeless. There were perhaps tens of thousands of them, and, as well as wondering what had gone wrong for them to be washed up like that, I selfishly worried about what would happen when they began to rot away. What would the smell of decomposing jellyfish be like? What would it look like; would there be a congealed mess smeared all over the beach for weeks? Oddly, the next day there was no sign of them, not even a damp mark left on the pebbles; apparently they had simply evaporated away.

The second was hearing a commotion of bird noise and coming out of the cabin just in time to see a large bird of prey followed by dozens of tiny birds – sparrows, finches, and robins – all scolding vigorously. The big bird flew out to sea, with the smaller birds in pursuit. The trail of small birds obscured my view of the bigger one, so I couldn't see what it was, though it was far bigger than any of them, and must have been either a buzzard or an eagle. At first it appeared to be enticing those tiny birds along behind it, like children following the Pied Piper. But then I realized that the larger bird was actually being mobbed by the smaller ones; they were chasing it away. They flew quite a distance out to sea and then, once confident they'd seen it off, flew back in small groups, and everything went quiet again.

One night I was woken in the early hours by the light. The sky was a rich and luminous blue, almost incandescent, streaked with gold-yellow clouds, through which golden light flowed downwards. It was light enough for a heron to be fishing on the beach. Everything was washed in golden radiance: the sand gilded, the pebbles glazed, and the sea gold-dazzled. Even the heron, strutting through the water, had a golden lustre.

They say the light and the colours that far north are different. This is a result of the plentiful rain washing impurities from the atmosphere; the air is rinsed clean, the light is pristine, and the colours of things are purified. It was like a pure land, a place of astonishing beauty. I fell in love; I had never been anywhere so enchanting.

The lochs and lochans were also places of strong presence and atmosphere. I would come through the wooded lowlands, up the beck, over the ridge of a hill and suddenly I was in the presence of the lake. It did feel like a *presence*, a slight, strange charge in the air, an uncanny feeling that something significant could happen, like walking into a room full of people who are all oddly silent. Where did that particular atmosphere come from?

It was, in part, the combined effect of the senses. All of a sudden I was in silence: the white noise, the rushing white, black, and tobacco yellow of the beck was behind me and the pool sat perfectly still and quiet. No birds sang. It was a quiet that cleansed, an almost disquieting quiet. There was a rush of emptiness in my ears; the mind reached out, searched round for some sound. But there was only the silence. This silence, this absence, simultaneously expanded me outside of myself, beyond the internal chatter, and also threw me back on myself; I became more aware of myself as a being, a creature, in a place, as a voice in a landscape. Where did that silence reside: 'inside' my mind, or 'out there' around the lake? It suddenly seemed to be not one or the other, nor both, nor neither.

The surface of the pool was pure peat-black and glittering. Or, on a fine sunny day, it shone like sapphire, or silver, or dark, dark blue. The colour was strong and pure, and yet reflective, and yet again diaphanous, so clean I saw right down into it. It appeared solid, and also liquid. This combination of qualities created suspense and strangeness. I was no longer quite sure what I was gazing at. Was it actually solid? Or was it, after all, liquid? Or was it made of some other substance, some other unknown element? It became a gap, a portal, a mysterious space, a thin place. The unfamiliar sensory world took my awareness somewhere new and different.

Walking up towards a ridge further east one day, it looked smooth and gently undulating, which led me to expect to be walking on easy, grassy slopes. But once on top I saw that the ridge was like rubble and it went on for miles: scree and stones, sometimes bigger slabs of rock, bone-grey, moon-white, like limestone. Later on, I learnt that the ridge was actually made from Cambrian quartzite, a white stone that weathers grey. It was geologically very different from the mountains nearer where I was staying, which were gritty, red-brown Torridonian sandstone. This made for mountains that were like 'stacks', tower-like, steeply rising with distinctive shapes, whilst the ridge I was walking on now was a sprawling heap of a mountain, with very different physical forms and textures, but still, in its own way, a dramatic, striking landscape.

As if a huge tipper truck had dumped the most enormous mounds of rubble, there was not merely a scattering of stones over underlying earth and solid rock, there was only rubble, just rubble, miles of rubble. The whole ridge appeared to be made of a heap of stones that stretched out as far as I could see. Occasionally there was a patch of moss, or perhaps a small tuft of wind-stunted thrift. Otherwise it was like a moonscape, strange and alien, and appearing lifeless, except that once or twice there was a sudden whir of white wings as a ptarmigan broke cover and sprinted away.

At the highest points of the ridge there were bigger rocks emerging out of the rubble, resembling the twisted and broken backbone of a monster whale. I wondered how such a mountain was made: what caused such a huge piling up of stone, like a whole town reduced to rubble, or an airport runway bombed to pieces, shards of tarmac ripped up and turned over?

It was tough walking, although my steps gradually tuned in to the terrain. The mind and the body worked in unison. This mind-body scrambled over the awkward rocks; each step involved a placing of the foot in a particular place and at a specific angle. The mind was nimble; it ran a few steps ahead of the body, faster than feet. Even as one foot was placed, the eyes were scanning ahead and the mind already had an idea where the next footstep was going. If I slipped, or a stone suddenly gave way, my foot instinctively skipped and regained balance. In the sensing body was the awareness of the mind; in the mind was the awareness of the body. And it all happened quicker than thought, or at least quicker than conscious thought. It wasn't 'me' doing the walking, not my conscious self that likes to think it is in control of the body. The mind-body had tuned in to the mountain; it danced to the rhythm of the rubble.

Often the more self-conscious part of my mind, that activity of mind I tend to identify as 'me', raced away. Like a dog off the leash it ran all around, darted hither and thither, sniffed about, dashed off urgently in one direction, then trotted back again wagging its tail. Sometimes it hankered after the past, sometimes tried to anticipate the future, or sometimes tried to grasp at the present. Scraps of a pop song I had not listened to for years, then an imaginary argument with someone from work, followed by a fantasy about meeting a beautiful woman: a stream of impressions tumbled through my mind. I talked to myself, 'It is amazing here, but what will be round the next curve in the path? Maybe there will be a view even more impressive.' My mind constantly told itself a story, the story of *me*, me and my adventures. But the irony was that the story prevented me from really being there, it inhibited a fuller, deeper sense of adventure. This place was so beautiful and yet somehow I was distracted, unable to be more totally present. I wanted to gather that beauty in my arms, but it slipped out of my grasp, it eluded and escaped me.

Gradually, however, the rhythm of walking lulled my thinking mind into quieter, deeper thought. The mind ambled rather than raced, wandered not worried. At the same time, the steady effort of walking kept the blood circulating, the energy flowing, and the mind alert and attentive.

The word 'mantra' means something like 'that which protects'. The idea behind a mantra is that, by repeatedly chanting sounds associated with a Buddha or bodhisattva,[3] the mind is protected. For the devotee the chanting involves orientating their mind, their intentions and aspirations, towards the spiritual qualities, the presence, of a higher power – an Enlightened being. But even on a basic psychological level we can see that the mantra, in a positive sense, 'distracts' the mind: the chanting occupies the mind so that there is no room left for the everyday anxieties and irritations that can be so self-proliferating. In this way, the mantra 'protects' the mind and makes it more wieldy, more ready and receptive to higher influences.

Walking, if you like, is akin to prayer or mantra. The steady rhythm, the refinement of the senses, the lift of energy, the working of mind and body in harmony: all this frees the mind, leaving space for deeper thoughts, moods, and images to rise to the surface. No wonder so many religions have traditions of pilgrimage; the physical act of walking can be just as prayerful as the rituals and observances undertaken at the final destination.

As I walked along that ridge, the surroundings refined my awareness. The way new views and vistas emerged opened out my mind, stimulated the senses without putting them on edge. The stippled stripes of scree on the hillsides soothed the senses without being soporific. I was taken further out of myself, expanded out of those self-encircled cycles of thought. My awareness became less driven, less urgent and utilitarian. And the world became more beautiful.

Beauty is a meeting, a mingling. It is an interaction. On my side, the side of the 'subject', there was a mind, and therefore a perception, that had become more sensitive and clear, more alive and engaged, though in a disinterested, non-utilitarian kind of way. Looked at in this fashion, things became more beautiful. Very ordinary things, even plain or 'ugly' rocks or puddles or scraps of moss, could become more interesting, and then more pleasing and beautiful. Beauty is a state of mind, a way of looking and listening.

But the other side, the side of the 'object', played its part too. Some things encourage and support this kind of perception more readily. These rock shapes and mountain forms were stimulating to the mind and senses, interesting, varied, subtle, engaging, but not overstimulating, not trying to grab or manipulate my attention, not triggering craving and grasping, just enjoyable and satisfying for their own sake. Beauty is not only in the eye of the beholder; some of what we look at supports and encourages the state of mind, the mode of perception, which allows for beauty, whilst other things we might encounter don't. Often the patterns and rhythms of nature do help us move in the direction of aesthetic appreciation.

In this co-arising of 'subject' and 'object' that is the process of perception, there is creativity. Perception involves selection from the mass of sensory data available at any given moment, and then interpretation and ordering of this data as influenced by memories, expectations, attitudes, interests, and so on. We are not just reproducing an objective representation of what is 'out there'. But nor are we imagining something entirely in the privacy of our own minds. Again, there is a mingling, a 'negotiation' between inner and outer. Each moment of perception is a kind of 'creation'; we are making something out of the raw material of the physical senses and the inner sense of mind. When we perceive beauty we have, in a sense, created beauty. We have created it in relationship, in collaboration, with the world around us. Every moment of perception is a moment of creativity, or at least potentially so. This creative power of the mind is inherently satisfying and enjoyable. The patterns, the harmony and order, we perceive in the world create a sense of harmony within us – the 'outer' and the 'inner' mirror each other.

In her classic work *The Living Mountain* Nan Shepherd writes:

Why some blocks of stone, hacked into violent and tortured shapes, should so profoundly tranquilise the mind I do not know. Perhaps the eye imposes its own rhythm on what is only a confusion: one has to look creatively to see this mass of rock as more than jag and pinnacle... A certain kind of consciousness interacts with the mountain-forms to create this sense of beauty. Yet the forms must be there for the eye to see. And forms of a certain distinction: mere dollops won't do it. It is, as with all creation, matter impregnated with mind: but the resultant tissue is a living spirit...[4]

I described this kind of perception as 'non-utilitarian' but I want to qualify that. I might consider a pile of stones, wanting to get on and build a drystone wall, and yet look with a sensitivity, receptivity, and openness to the shapes of the stones and the possibilities they offer. There can be a utilitarian awareness of things that is still appreciative and sensitive. If I didn't look this way, if I rushed to get the job done, it would be done badly. It is the driven, grasping mind that takes us out of that more intimate relationship with the world.

There was, for me, another significant discovery during this retreat in the far north, one that has stayed with me and that I try to remember and stay connected to, even once back from a solitary retreat and immersed again in my 'ordinary' life. On my first full day on that retreat in the Highlands I hid my watch away. I had experimented with this before; I liked living for a while by 'organic' time, rather than being driven by 'clock' time. On this retreat I decided to try it again, which, since I was there for a whole month, meant trying it for a much longer period. I put my watch down in the bottom of a drawer. Now I could let things take time, let them take the time they take. I could eat when I was hungry, sleep when I was tired. As Henry Thoreau said:

> It matters not what the clocks say or the attitude and labors of men. Morning is when I am awake and there is a dawn in me.[5]

I knew that in my life back home I was often, maybe subconsciously, hurrying to get things done by a certain time. This hurrying is still a tendency of mine. Sometimes it is necessary for practical reasons, but often it can be because I get stuck in a habit, a mode of rushing. During that summer month in Scotland I began to see more clearly how I could become perpetually pitted against time. I treated time like a container, separate from me, into which I would try and stuff as many activities and experiences as possible. My day could then end up resembling a hastily overpacked suitcase, stuffed full, and consequently so messy and jumbled that I sometimes couldn't find what I needed. I would mistakenly equate getting things done quicker, getting the to-do list all ticked off, with having more time to do what I really wanted to do. But it never quite worked like that.

How I spent my time determined how fast or slow time paid me back. If I raced against time, wanting to get more done, then time raced too, it ran swiftly into the distance. If I wanted the time to pass quickly, because I was bored and feeling empty or dull, then time dragged its feet. Time went at a quick march or else at a snail's pace; it shifted gear, accelerated and decelerated. My *idea* of time back then was of something uniform, even, external, and objective. But my *experience* of time was variable, uneven, inward, and subjective. That experience of time was conditioned by the quality of my awareness, and then tended to reinforce and perpetuate that mode, or quality, of awareness. It was mind-made; it was a kind of mental elastic that could stretch or contract. So I was able to appreciate that a particular state of mind is also a particular state of time. Our attitudes towards time and our actual experience of time are intertwined. For time is not something we are *in*; it is something that we *are*.

But if, instead of rushing, I was able to be absorbed in the beauty around me, peaceful and content, I could flow along with time, allow things to unfold at their own pace. The effect of this was that I forgot about time – it stretched and opened out, almost into timelessness, into eternity. Craving or aversion made time oppressive and domineering, marching to the tick-tock of the clock. Letting go of craving was also a loosening of time, a quietening of that insistent tick-tocking.

The isolated little beach and that rocky coastline in the far north had perhaps a stronger effect on me than anywhere I had been before. I spent hours sitting on rocks just watching, gazing at the ocean and its birds, captivated by the spacious blues of sea and sky, and the beautiful, golden aura of the sun. Time began to have a very different quality. We all experience this, or at least hints of it. Perhaps, for example, we are in a new and stimulating environment, travelling in a different country, and we feel after a few days that we have been there for weeks. My experience – and

I know it is also that of many others – is that a retreat can be even more like this. To be more aware is to be more alive, to have more life, and so, in a sense, to have more time – certainly a deeper, richer experience that manifests as a folding out of time. To be more mindful is to be more time-full, to live longer.

I could see that my day-to-day life could often be geared to getting – acquiring things, doing tasks and projects, arriving at a destination on time. This meant always looking to the future, and the result was that restlessness and discontentment, a sense of never ever fully arriving, could be intrinsic to my experience. Happiness and contentment were found only when I could be truly and fully in the present. To push against that present moment elongated time. To grasp at the moment compressed it. To just be in the moment unravelled and released it. It wasn't time in itself that was the problem, more my craving and my striving against time, my mistaken idea that time was a fixed-volume container, and the more I could cram into it, the happier I would be.

I am sure it is also possible to do practical things, even to do them quickly and with an awareness of time, whilst remaining in the moment. However, when away from it all, with no practical need to keep to clock time, I found hiding my watch away was liberating. It allowed me to forget about time, which undermined the tendency to strive to fit more in, and helped me to stay more fully in the present. It was still surprising, however, how tempting it could be to dig my watch out from that drawer and sneak a look. For some strange reason knowing the 'proper' time seemed to give a sense of security. This was partly a slight underlying anxiety that I could lose count of the days, lose track of time, and not know when I was due to go home again! But there was also, for the first few days, something else: a vague, unsettling sense of unease that showed me just how much I defined myself, located myself, in time. Was it force of habit, an undertow of worry about missing a deadline, or being late for an appointment? But here there were no deadlines, and the only appointment I had was with my own self.

The discomfort of not knowing the time showed me how I measured myself by the clock, how this gave me a sense of security, of reassurance, of self-justification. The relative 'success' or 'failure' of my hours and days was judged – subtly and subconsciously – by how much I had got done, and how much time it had taken. I could see that although I was trying not to live by clock time it continued ticking away inside my head. It was as if, although I'd stopped winding up the clock, it still took a few days to fully wind down.

Of course, although I had dispensed with my watch and conventional clock time, there was still 'natural' time; one gets a rough sense of the progress of the day from the position of the sun in the sky. But up here in the far north, in the midsummer, there wasn't the usual, familiar rough correspondence between clock time and natural time. The sun circled the whole heaven, and only just, after midnight, arced under the ocean's horizon, so that it never really grew dark. Sometimes, I suspect, I ended up keeping rather strange hours: having breakfast around lunchtime, going for my afternoon walk in the evening, and eating my evening meal way past my usual bedtime. It was much harder to judge the time of day. In fact, this experience highlighted the relative, contingent nature of concepts like 'the time of day', or 'breakfast time'. It accentuated the sense of timelessness. I gained an even stronger sense of expansiveness and openness in time.

Living largely out of doors, I was more aware of the sun tracking through the sky. I would often watch the sunset, or the sunrise not long after. As is the case from wherever in the world you watch the sunset or sunrise, the sun looked as if it was moving quicker. It was an optical illusion of course, caused by the sun's proximity to the horizon, giving me a reference point with which to gauge its movement through the sky. Its rising or falling became more perceptible. The colours of the light – gold, orange, purple-red – also changed more swiftly and dramatically, compared to the more uniform hue of the daytime sky. The temperature shifted more suddenly.

All this created a sense of time and transition. I was physically, sensorially, in time, witnessing time. Something strange then happened to that time; it seemed to simultaneously speed up and slow down. The journey of the sun appeared faster, quickening the sense of transition. Another day was over, gone for ever. Or another day was being born. But also, witnessing that transition, being so absorbed in it, slowed me down. There was a hush, a pause, a sense of being suspended in between one day and another. I could become more aware of time's passing and its preciousness. Sometimes something would click into place; I would be flowing along with time, I could let go into the unfolding moment, rather than being in my usual mode of tussling with time. To flow with time is to forget time. Living in the land of the midnight sun accentuated that sense of timelessness.

Looking back, I can see that this particular retreat marked a staging post; it was a turning point in how I spent my times of solitude. The natural environment became even more important than before. That sense of place took on an even greater significance. The beauty of the far north had moved me, stilled me; I had touched down into deeper sources of contentment.

Previously, I had enjoyed the overall experience of solitude, though within that would be plenty of ups and downs: restlessness or boredom, despondency or distraction, followed by rapturous inspiration or almost ecstatic joy – all sometimes in the course of a single day. This time I had settled into a still, steady, more even-keeled happiness and contentment. Previously, by the end of a solitary retreat I would feel it had been good, but I was definitely ready to go home. This time I felt I could have happily stayed on for longer.

4

Through the green gate

A few years after my time in Scotland I had the opportunity to stay for a while in a cottage in the rugged hill-farming county of Cumbria. The fells of the Lake District shouldered together on the horizon, whilst the land nearer by was like a knobbly old man, dressed in plushest green velvet. The house where I was staying was named Waingap Cottage. It was a mile up an undulating lane, at a point where, as described by the cottage's name, the road narrowed and there was only enough width for a single vehicle to pass.

One day I was hurrying back along the lane, thumping up the hump of the hill with two heavy bags of shopping. What with the gradient of the hill and the weight of the bags, I was eager to get home, and not paying much attention to my surroundings. I was striding along in a world of my own.

As I came round a bend in the road, however, something in the corner of my eye caught my attention. I'd startled a bird off a stone wall. It was blue on top, red below, quite brightly coloured. I stopped and turned, curious to know what it was. What followed took place in less than five seconds. It was one of those experiences – like an accident occurring, or hearing a shocking piece of news – in which the mind suddenly shifts gear. Time slowed right down and I saw each distinct instant of consciousness, each particular moment of perception, each individual thought, as it came and went.

My first thought – given the colours of the bird and its proximity to a stream – was 'kingfisher'. My second thought was the realization that it was far too big to be a kingfisher. My mind scrabbled to recognize, categorize. Third thought: it is flying straight at me. Fourth thought: what can it possibly be?

It flew fast, propelling itself powerfully through the space between us. I noticed each wingbeat, and how, as its wings drummed back, its body surged forward. It was not a big bird, but that made the sheer speed of its flight more striking. It was like watching a strong rower who, with each pull on the oars, slices the boat faster through the water. In no time it had flown within a foot of my face. I could clearly see the yellow of its eye, with its black centre and its burning, fierce, stare. It was at that moment that my scrambling mind produced a fifth thought that finally identified it: sparrowhawk! I yelled out loud and pulled my head back. In the same instant the hawk banked in the opposite direction, hurtling over the hedgerow.

Involuntarily I stepped back a few more paces. I was – quite literally – taken aback. I stepped back in amazement, still holding my bags of shopping. The bird, which from the colours of its plumage I now knew to be a male sparrowhawk, had shocked me out of my daydreamer state. I was now wide awake. He had startled me to my senses, jolted me into alertness, amazed me back into the world. Someone later suggested that the hawk might also have been sleeping. It is very unlikely a sparrowhawk would fly at someone like that deliberately. Perhaps I'd caught him off guard too as I'd come quickly round the corner of the quiet lane. It had certainly felt like it for that instant we'd stared at each other; there was something of a surprised look in the glare of his eye.

The yellow glare of that eye: it was still burning into my mind hours, even days, later. I couldn't fully explain it, but that encounter felt special and significant, even like a kind of 'blessing'. I had been turned back to myself, confronted and challenged by a creature from a different dimension, one that was wild and animal. I lived my human life, in my human world, but there were other lives, other ways of being, other possible modes of awareness too. The encounter made me more aware of an animal itself, in and for itself, as a creature as alive and aware as I am. Part of the effect of this was to make me more aware of *myself* as animal too, with my particular sense faculties and mode of awareness.

Another morning at Waingap I was sitting enjoying a leisurely breakfast, watching the world outside the kitchen window. Across the garden was an old stone wall. All along it were dense mats of moss, whole moss forests, and scabby crusts of lichen, calcite-grey and sulphur-yellow. In the middle, in a gap in the wall, was a rusty iron gate. Through the gate was a field, which sloped away to the farm below.

Up the hill came a fox. It crept, step by careful step, eyes fixed hard ahead, ears on edge. Every hair and muscle on its body prickled with nervous energy. This was a fox on red alert, an electric fox, ready to pounce. Suddenly there was a blur of brown across the gap in the wall. A rabbit ran for its life, with the fox in hot pursuit.

Britain is not a large island, and it is mostly densely populated and developed by humans. We've domesticated virtually the whole country. What animals and birds there are can seem familiar and ordinary. We know what they are, we know their names, and we can think we know all about them. But do we really know them? Know what they eat, when they sleep, how they raise their young, where they die? How much of their lives do we really see, other than a fleeting glimpse?

To see a fox is not unusual; they are commonplace, even in the urban environment. But this was a fox as I'd not encountered one before, a fox in all its bristling, raw, hunger-driven animal-ness.

I felt that hot fox energy, pulsing through every fibre of its body. I got closer up to its non-human awareness and presence. It was as if the rusty gate had swung open and allowed me a glimpse through into another world. That gap in the wall had become an entry point through which I'd seen something of the animal life going on every day: of hunting or being hunted, eating or being eaten, surviving and living, or succumbing and dying. For a fleeting moment I'd been on the threshold of the animal realm. It was like when I had encountered the sparrowhawk. Somehow it felt like an honour, a privilege, something precious.

In his poem 'Roe-deer', Ted Hughes writes of being out in the wintry dawn and coming across two deer on a road through some woods. In those few moments, as he watches, and the deer stare back at him, something strange seems to happen:

> I could think the deer were waiting for me
> To remember the password and the sign
>
> That the curtain had blown aside for a moment
> And there where the trees were no longer trees,
>   nor the road a road
>
> The deer had come for me.[6]

Places in nature, or encounters with wild creatures, can be enchanting. We've set foot in a fairy-tale land. We've accidentally stumbled into a secret world that only comes alive when humans are not looking. We've been granted entrance into a magical place that we never dreamt existed. It is as if 'the curtain had blown aside for a moment' and another world and its creatures are waiting for us. It is akin to an 'initiation': our idea of world is expanded, becomes more alive and extraordinary than we realized. We are beckoned over the borders into a new realm. The boundaries between our world and the wild world become more diaphanous. We are in *their* place, and this feels magical and privileged. Whilst the experience may be only brief, these moments become jewel-like, crystallizations of joy, wonder, or even love, treasured even years later. When we tell our friends about them, they often respond by recounting stories of their own, delightedly telling us of the time they were touched by the wild. These meetings seem to matter deeply to us all – they feel significant and important.

Another day, up the lane beyond the cottage, walking the footpaths over the fields, I came across some cattle. This was a different kind of meeting. They were not wild creatures, but nor were they entirely domesticated. They had yet another kind of awareness, not so fiercely independent and suspicious, but not familiar and trusting either. They might have been farm animals, and somewhat used to humans, but still I was unknown and unexpected. One cow was lowing; to my ears her voice sounded mournful, a moaning from her heavy heart, patient but plaintive, pleading. Another cow, as I got near, stopped grazing and lifted her head. She raised it slowly, as if it was heavy. Her ears, erect at ninety degrees, swivelled my way like security cameras. The nostrils dilated and moistened, and she sniffed and sucked in air. The eyes were mute, careful looking. She just stood still and stared. She looked perplexed, as if I was a puzzle. I wondered what she was experiencing, what her senses were telling her, what she smelt and saw. I talked to her, but was met with blank incomprehension, even though I was only trying to communicate a peaceful intention. More silence. Then the stocky head slowly lowered back to earth again, her nose back in the spiky twists of grass, her tongue gathering it in, teeth tugging at the turf with that lush, satisfying ripping sound of animal grazing.

Over the stile and into the next field and there was a herd of bullocks. They came thudding up with the curiosity of children, sniffing with slobbered noses, boyish and boisterous, and then slow and shy as they reached me. They looked at me, and then at each other, wondering what to do. Suddenly, as if at some invisible signal, they pushed and shoved at each other, and went stomping away.

Further up, in the corner of a field, sat a bull. His coat was fawn with a pinkish bloom, the colour of fallen oak leaves in autumn. On his heavy neck and head the hair was curled. He sat with front hoofs folded under the massive body; he had the stature of a lion, only with more weight. Anything he might lack in fire, he made up for in earth. As I passed by carefully, almost reverentially, just one eye flickered my way for a second. Otherwise he ignored me, unblinking, not chewing the cud, tail not even bothered to flick at flies on the mound of his back. He simply rested: so solid, still, and solemn.

Walking back down that lane I saw two deer through a gap in the hedge. They were small deer, their coats varying in colour from silver to dark grey-brown, with a blue-grey sheen like the fur of a Persian blue cat. Their ears were edged with black. They had that tipped-up look of deer, with their long back legs and powerful rear muscles. They were both does, and were grazing, but every few seconds looked up and listened. I stood still by the gate and watched, wondering whether, if I waited patiently and quietly enough, they might come closer. They carried on grazing, jerking their heads up and checking around them every few seconds. Their necks were supple, turning elegantly in any direction.

The cold started to soak up into me; I could feel it like iced acid, stinging my feet. But their grazing did gradually bring the deer my way. Then one of them seemed to notice me and actually started walking towards me. She was staring at me, wide-eyed. Her ears were perked and pointed in my direction. She sniffed the air, curious, and came up closer. Then she continued to graze, though continually looking up again. It was as if she couldn't quite believe her eyes, like I was some strange apparition, and that if she were to turn away for a moment, and then look back, I wouldn't really be there. We carried on like that for several minutes, watching each other, and wondering. Eventually I did have to move my stiffening limbs and immediately both deer bolted.

Even in a managed and cultivated countryside like this, there could be such encounters: those moments when I straddled two worlds, where a creature and I met each other and stopped and stared, wondering and curious. Two paths converged, and those times and places seemed special, even magical. Those chance meetings triggered delight and amazement and would be cherished and remembered for years to come. There could be an element of surprise, as though the creature and I had astonished each other into a different kind of awareness. And there could be a sense of 'otherness', or strangeness. They – and perhaps I too – hovered on the borderlands between curiosity and fear. From their point of view I should not have been there; *I* was the one from another dimension.

From my side, I became more aware of them as a *creature*, more aware of them being aware. Their sense faculties and awareness are so different from mine; how can I imagine what they are experiencing? They and their world remain something of a mystery to me. I reflected that, although these creatures were not aware in the same way that I was, they certainly were aware and alive, and that awareness is, in its own way, extraordinary. Closely observing the creatures around Waingap in this way kindled a sense of empathy and connection.

As David Abram writes in *The Spell of the Sensuous*:

all of the creativity and free-ranging mobility that we have come to associate with the human intellect is, in truth, an elaboration, or recapitulation, of a profound creativity already underway at the most immediate level of sensory perception. The sensing body is not a programmed machine but an active and open form [...] If the body were truly a set of closed or predetermined mechanisms, it could never come into contact with anything outside of itself, could never perceive anything new, could never be genuinely startled or surprised. All of its experience [...] would already have been anticipated from the beginning [...] But could we even, then, call them experiences? For is not experience, or more precisely, *perception*, the constant thwarting of such closure?[7]

I remember watching a squirrel in some woods. A bird feeder, full of peanuts, had been hung on a few metres of wire from a branch of an oak tree. The arrangement was obviously designed to keep out squirrels. But it was winter and perhaps the squirrel was very hungry; it was certainly determined to find a way to get to the nuts. It scrabbled up and down the trunk of the tree, testing the distance between it and the feeder. It crouched upright, head down, sideways, at all angles, to see if it made any difference. Then it scurried around the nearest branches, down this one, along that, trying to find a way across, or at least determine the nearest point. It even tried hanging down, stretching its body, and reaching out its paws as far as it could. All this went on for ten minutes, and then it came down the trunk of the tree again, scrambling about, eyeing up the space between it and a good meal. Several times it tensed as if to jump, but then seemed to think the distance too far and changed its mind. Then there was a particularly long pause, the squirrel's body taut, before it leapt and landed on the bird feeder. I couldn't help but applaud and laugh out loud; I felt glad that its industry and inventiveness had been rewarded.

Whilst spending a lot of time in the wild Abram noticed that his sensing of the world, or his awareness of what was going on with another creature, was felt in his own body. He came to think that when we are truly sensitive our bodies have a kind of sympathetic response that augments the perception, and that is, in truth, another aspect of that perception. This empathic awareness is in the senses and in the body. I was taken aback by the sparrowhawk; I literally stepped back a few paces after it had gone. I felt the amazement in my body; I was shocked to a standstill. Watching the fox creep up the hillside I tensed as it tensed, preparing to pounce on the rabbit. Watching the squirrel scrabble round the tree, I felt its frustration; suspense prickled round my body and instinctively I held my breath. And I felt a release, a little rush of energy and elation, and I exhaled again, when it landed safely on the feeder. I experienced a more *participative*, sympathetic awareness.

I realized that, whilst I was living here at Waingap, I was tuning in to my surroundings in a very particular way. There was a train line and station a couple of miles from the cottage. Sometimes I could hear the train; it sounded distant but also surprisingly clear. I realized that, when it was audible, this meant the wind was coming from the east, which probably meant colder, dryer weather. If I couldn't hear the train at all, this told me that the wind was from the west, and most likely warmer, wetter weather was on the way. But what was interesting was that this awareness had developed quite instinctively. I hadn't consciously made the association, nor was I deliberately listening out for the sound of the train. It was a more innate, naturally made, connection. It was a very simple and, in many ways, unremarkable thing. But it mattered to me. Though the noise of the train wasn't a natural sound, I welcomed it; it became familiar, part of things, like the voice of a friend calling from afar. I realized that I loved being attuned to my surroundings in this way. I had a strong and heartfelt wish to belong. The strength of this desire took me by surprise; it meant so much to me to know intimately the land where I dwelt, and to sense my place in it. I longed for that more participative way of being. Feeling so earthed and grounded, located and connected, was a new experience for me, and, at the same time, it seemed deeply instinctual and long-buried.

In some ways I felt more rooted in, and connected to, the world when at Waingap than I had felt anywhere else. Through becoming so familiar with those lanes and fields, and through the various encounters I had there, my heart had opened as never before. Barriers had come down; my sense of being a self that was separated off from the world, isolated 'in here', had attenuated and softened to some extent. I was closer to life, and this felt right and good.

I was here at Waingap through the autumn and into the winter, and it was another time of change in my life. I had given up being director of the Buddhist centre back home, after eight years working hard and long hours in that job. It felt like the end of a significant phase. It hadn't just been a job, but more of a vocation and a whole way of life. It had, on the whole, been a tremendously inspired and creative time, to which I'd felt totally dedicated and committed. But I had run out of steam. I had noticed myself longing for a different quality in my life. The word I used to encapsulate this back then was 'simplicity'. During this phase I remember once looking round at an exhibition of paintings in the local arts centre back home. I came to one painting of a cottage on a cliff overlooking the sea. My heart did a leap. Something physically moved inside me towards the painting and what it represented. My heart was telling me something. I knew that it would be dangerous not to listen.

So I had moved on and had come away to review my life, not to a cottage on a cliff top, but to one in the rugged Cumbrian landscape. It wasn't an unbroken stretch of solitude – a number of friends came to visit me. I enjoyed those visits and was pleased to show them the places I'd grown to love. But, although it could be delightful to share a walk in the wild with friends, there was something different and unique about being there alone. It was easier to be quiet, to just be, and this allowed me to get closer up and closer in to nature. I couldn't help feeling a little bit relieved after they had gone, and I was by myself again. I would stroll back up the lane, to check what had happened, to see what had changed, in the days since I had last walked that way. It was as if I was reconnecting, like I was calling in on each tree, each field, each lane, to say hello. I was back where I belonged.

Previous solitary retreats had been about stepping back a little way, in order to regain inspiration and energy, and then to go back home, re-engaged with my work and my life. This time I was stepping back further and more radically. I was, in a way, taking stock of the whole of my early adulthood. I felt very fortunate to have the opportunity to do this, and to be able to take time out in such a beautiful place.

As I looked back and reviewed that period of my life I could see the inevitable mixture of successes and failures, satisfactions and disappointments, alliances and conflicts. There were also certain painful thoughts and emotions I was trying to avoid. I became uncomfortably aware of how bound up my identity and sense of self-worth were with the role I had relinquished. The solitude exacerbated that awareness. I saw that this is one of the points of undertaking a solitary retreat: to touch down into one's basic aloneness and to experience oneself free of role, status, or job title. But on this occasion I wasn't just temporarily leaving my identity behind. I had actually given up that old life. Here, all alone, it was brought home to me even more forcibly how much I had invested in that identity. It was, of course, entirely human and understandable, especially in someone relatively young, but the strength of feeling still surprised me.

I was also thinking about what to do next. I felt pulled in different directions, and was in that awkward period of having left behind one way of life but not yet having found a new one. I was floating in a vacuum, suspended in an empty gap. I sometimes entered periods of doubt and despondency, my past catching up with me whilst I faced into the uncertainty of the future.

It was January and there was a week or so of heavy fog. The weather was cold and leaden and it seemed that an air of confusion obscured and shrouded the hills. The far-off mountains no longer existed. I walked up the lane peering into the dull grey mist. Everything was shrunken in and flattened, amorphous and monochrome. The skeletal trees looked cold, metallic. Last summer's bracken lay broken, rusting by the roadside. A mesh of brambles hung limp over the bracken. A wren worried amidst this wreckage of summer. Leaves were mashed to a mess of mud by the wheels of a tractor. The dips in the hills had become pockets of charcoal darkness, regions where frost never thawed, but remained on the fields like ash. I couldn't see more than a few yards ahead. All of this matched my mood. And it helped me turn inwards; I needed to face the internal weather.

A deeper shift was taking place. My previous life had been rich and rewarding, but it had also been constantly busy, chaotic, changing, disrupted, all through my own volition. It – I – was overdriven, and as soon as one thing was finished I was on to the next. There was, of course, a connection between this perpetual busyness and the investment and overidentification with the role.

Now I wanted something less complex and driven. My old life had got me to where I was; I wasn't regretting the past or repudiating it. I didn't feel like I had failed, more that an old way of being had had its time and was now no longer helpful. No doubt it had a lot to do with getting older. Something else in me was longing for expression. Temperamentally I tend to be quiet and reserved, and my inner world is extremely important to me. But I also have this active and idealistic side that wants to express that inner landscape more outwardly. I am also quite capable and practical and therefore, in those days, I tended to end up in positions of responsibility, busy with administration and detail, and needing to deal constantly with matters in the external world. I was an introvert who seemed to always end up right in the middle of things, and this had become too much of a strain.

What happened during my time at Waingap supported and augmented this realization. There was a connection between my desire for a less complex, busy life, and what I discovered here about that more participative awareness in a place and with the creatures inhabiting it. So often my heart and mind could be guarded and closed against what I didn't want or like, or tightened and contracted around what I felt anxious about. The desire to be in more intimate relationship to my surroundings was an expression and extension of the wish for simplicity.

I felt I had deepened and continued the learning of my previous retreat up in the far north of Scotland. Life can be busy; modern life can be especially overloaded with input and stimulation. Often I didn't give myself time to process and assimilate, and the result was that, subtly and subconsciously, I couldn't deal with the input and pushed it aside in my mind, dulling the heart down further. But in this place I had the time and conditions for my heart to really open, open as wide as the view from the hilltops. The heart needs time, needs space. The process of watching, listening, noticing – of really being in this place – led to love, to a strongly felt heart connection.

This empathy didn't arise automatically, just through me planting myself in some woodland, or herding myself up a mountain. As George Eliot once said, 'selfish instincts are not subdued by the sight of buttercups.'[8] It required willingness, a certain kind of effort, or intention, to really, fully be there. I needed to be open and receptive, attentive and appreciative. I needed to get myself out of the way, so that beauty had room to flower.

In the past I would have gone for a walk most days on my retreats. The walk would, however, have been primarily for exercise, for a break and rest from meditation or study. The real business of the retreat would have taken place on the meditation cushion. This had now changed. The wandering of the lanes and watching the creatures there: all this was now much more central to the retreat. It was a matter of *love*. That empathic and participative awareness: this was what counted more than anything else.

I had always thought of retreats as times for 'going in', for turning away from the world, tuning in to my inner life, and examining my own thoughts and feelings. Introspection, being inward-looking, was my reason for being alone. But, from this time on, my times of solitude became just as much about 'going out'. I wanted to turn out to the world, attune myself to my surroundings. I longed for a deeper connection, for familiarity and intimacy, with the places I stayed in. I spent less time on my retreats meditating, and more time ranging about in the woods and fields around me. I slept out on mountain tops. I sat gazing for hours at the waves on the sea. I felt an increasingly strong, heartfelt, even passionate, bond with some of those places.

At first I worried that this new approach was just an excuse for distracting myself, for giving free rein to restlessness so I could avoid facing myself and the contents of my mind. But my intuition told me that this wasn't the case, and that my newfound love and connection with nature was, for me, a significant development. The importance of this 'going out' increased over the years. I wanted to 'turn out' just as much as 'turn in', and the turning out seemed to be part of turning in, and vice versa.[9] They were a deepening of each other.

However, I was running out of money and needed to go back to 'ordinary life' again. My partner came to pick me and my belongings up. With kindness and sensitivity she offered to drive the car about a mile down to the bottom of the lane, and to wait for me there, allowing me to walk slowly, by myself, away from this place that had been so special and meaningful to me, and giving me time to say goodbye.

There is a story about the Buddha, in the weeks immediately after his Enlightenment, remaining in the same spot near the peepul tree close by the Niranjana River, absorbing and coming to terms with his awakening experience. It is said that when he finally got up to leave, to begin a new life teaching others how to find the same freedom that he had just discovered, he turned and bowed in gratitude to the tree. In that beautiful place, by the broad-flowing river, the tree had sheltered him from the hot suns, and from the monsoon rains. The tree and its surroundings had helped to make possible his extraordinary breakthrough; they had even become like companions during those crucial weeks of awakening and discovery.

For me, walking down that lane was a more gradual, gentle way of leaving than just driving off in a car. There was time to say goodbye. I felt so deeply for that place and what I had gained from being there that I found myself turning back, palms pressed together and held to my heart, bowing down in gratitude to the hills and hedgerows, to that landscape and its creatures, and to the beauty of nature.

I had a new job, was back in connection with my old friends and social circle, and moved to a small town on the edge of the city where I used to live. This town had suffered somewhat from disastrous town planning in the 1960s. Right round the heart of the town was an ugly, suffocating ring road known to locals as the 'concrete collar'. I was walking into town one day, approaching the ring road at a point where there was also a multistorey car park made of slabs of industrial concrete, and a council swimming pool, cheaply built and ugly. People I passed by looked bored, vacant. I was finding it difficult being back in the urban environment, and struggling to some extent to connect with my new life. In that moment I quite physically, tangibly felt myself 'closing down'. It was like a portcullis slammed shut round my heart, in an attempt to keep out everything I didn't want to be exposed to. That sense of participative awareness I'd felt at Waingap was gone.

It was a strong, very definite, experience; I can remember the exact place along the street that it happened. The mind-made barriers between self and world might have been lowered down whilst living at Waingap, but they were now firmly erected again. It was painful and regrettable that, however much my awareness had changed on retreat, it was now reverting. I couldn't sustain the consciousness I'd experienced in nature now I was back in the city. I was closing back down in to my usual, habitual mode: head down, just getting where I wanted to, as quick as I could. But I didn't want it to be like that: a brief, sporadic waking up, and then back to sleepwalking the dull treadmill again. I wanted to learn to stay open and alive even whilst in the city. Was this possible? I realized that this was the real challenge.

A couple of weeks later I was walking into town again and a strange thing happened. At exactly the same place where I'd had the 'closing down' experience I noticed something moving out of the corner of my eye. There was something familiar about its style: agile and dashing. I quickly looked up, surprised and delighted. A bird was flying, head down, shimmer-winged, low over the garden fences. I saw the mussel-blue of its back as it arced over a rooftop. It was a sparrowhawk.

5

A murder of crows

A few years later, after a particularly busy and demanding period in my life, I was able to do a solitary retreat at a place called Trwyn (pronounced 'true-win', with the emphasis on the first syllable). This was situated right at the mouth of an estuary in north-west Wales, with a view of hills and mountains in the distance. Trwyn was once a ferryman's cottage; the ferryman would have transported people over the mile-wide estuary to the town opposite, so that they could avoid either the long route round, or else having to wait till the tide was low enough to walk across the sands.

The ferry service had disappeared generations ago, though the town still thrived. At night orange street lights twinkled at me across the water. One friend of mine who'd done a retreat here wasn't too keen on the place because of the town being so close by and clearly visible. I could understand that, but I didn't mind so much. A mile was distance enough and, in a way, I liked looking across and being reminded of the world carrying on, business as usual, whilst I immersed myself in retreat. Occasionally people walked across the sands and along the beach, and they would peer up at the little cottage, curious. But no one came right up, as I'd heard had happened to other people who'd stayed there. So I felt away from it all and undisturbed, which was what I wanted.

Trwyn means 'nose' and, if one imagined taking a bird's-eye view, then the estuary was like a mouth, and Trwyn was on a little promontory like a nose sticking out above the mouth. Although extending outwards in this way, the land was wooded and the cottage was right round on one side of the promontory. This meant it didn't feel exposed, but quite private and tucked away.

I was able to stay there thanks to a friend who lived nearby and who had told me about the place and had taken me down to see it about a year previously. I loved the little cottage. It was stone-built, with rough and uneven stone flags on the floor, a wooden beamed ceiling, and some steps that went up to a gap in the ceiling to an attic room where I would meditate. I had to bring in all my food on foot, since the nearest road was a mile away, though somehow the cottage had been connected to the mains water and electricity supplies. I shared the cottage with a family of mice. Outside, a song thrush came and sung in a nearby tree most evenings. Out of the undergrowth came the babbling song of a blackcap, seeming so excited that he couldn't sound the words quick enough.

There was a male blackbird that came to bathe in a tub of water that filled from the gutters. I'd watch him preening himself afterwards. At first the vigour with which he stuck his head under his wing and poked at his feathers made it seem rough and haphazard. But if I watched closely I saw how thorough and precise he was. His beak picked out a feather and then ran down it whilst slightly, but very rapidly, opening and closing the beak. He quite neatly and carefully combed feather after feather in this way. Sometimes he did scratch rigorously at the back of his head with a claw, all the while looking at me, a bit suspicious. But he looked so dapper, so sharp-suited in that glossy black coat, with his smart orange bill, and his bright, attentive eyes.

Just a couple of yards out at the front of the cottage was a stone wall, and on the other side of this were rocks and rock pools, and then the open, ever-changing, space of the estuary.

When the tide was up it was like looking across a big lake. A few hours later it was a huge expanse of sand. I could just make out the sea on the horizon; I'd guess it was about two miles away. Then the water crept and curled back along the sandy channels, approaching with a steady inevitability. The incoming tide slid silently and sinuously. It came stealthily like a creature stalking its prey. Then it spread out like molten glass.

The estuary was saturated with life. This became most apparent as the tide approached. The incoming water brought life; it revived and renewed what had become dead and dried out, it revealed and returned what had got buried and hidden away. Slumps of seaweed lay sleeping, corpse-like, blackest green, dry and brittle, until the sea water softened them, gilded them brown-green with a gold-amber lustre. They were soaked back into a strange, eerie life. Woken up by the sea, lifted back upright, they began to dance: wraiths swaying to the rhythm of the water.

As the tide advanced, the sand slurped, sucked, and squirted. It was alive, hissing and spluttering. Little jets of sand would shoot ten inches into the air as creatures down below sensed the encroaching water. If you looked into the film of water as it moved up and spread out, you saw that it was oozing with hundreds of miniscule, semi-transparent shrimp-like creatures, tiny fish that were little more than two pinhead eyes with a tail, and larger crabs and gobies.

Then came birds. Redshanks tiptoed to and fro, poking and probing. Merganser ducks swam on the water dipping their heads under, peering to see if it was worth a dive. Cormorants just went straight in – doing their forward jump from a stationary position on the sea's surface, like a fish flipping into the water. Gulls lurked opportunistically – hanging around a merganser, and, if it caught anything, harassing it and trying to steal its catch. A couple of times I saw an osprey further out hunting for fish.

To me, watching from the cottage, the estuary was alive and attractive. I've read that the ancient Indians regarded that which was ever changing as inherently beautiful – always fresh, always new, never growing stale and old. Each successive moment would be unique, transporting the viewer into a timeless realm.[10] The estuary was certainly always changing. The turning tide, the flocks of birds ebbing and flowing, the playing of light on the water, the patterning of the clouds in the open sky, the sun setting in the evening – all was constantly shifting and moving. There was always something to look at that was different from yesterday, new and interesting. I found Trwyn an easy, soothing place to be; it absorbed me, it was generous and abundant, it gave beauty and contentment. Watching the tide was like following the sensations of inhaling and exhaling whilst meditating; the estuary was like a giant lung, slowly breathing in, and then breathing out again.

There is a growing body of research on the beneficial effects of nature on the quality of our awareness and attention. Links have been made between attention-deficit disorders in children and highly artificial and overstimulating environments that demand a certain kind of forced attention. In nature, by contrast, attention can be more relaxed and natural.[11] Because nature can help our attention and awareness in this way, it can support us into a more subtle, refined, meditative consciousness, where anxiety and craving can diminish to some extent.

Like many natural environments, this place was full of patterns that eddied and evolved, yet with endless subtle variation, never exactly repeating themselves. The sunlight laughing with the water, the ash leaves flirting with the wind, or the colourful patchwork of pebbles on the shoreline were restful yet stimulating, allowing my senses to relax, yet keeping them alert and alive. There was music, sculpture, and dance: the swash and sigh of the sea, or the rucks and wrinkles carved in sand as the tide receded, or the way the tall grasses bobbed and bowed to each other in the wind. Nature's patterns lay somewhere between order and chaos, neither uniform and predictable, nor random and incomprehensible.

One of Hans Christian Andersen's tales tells of a Chinese emperor who loves the song of the nightingale that sings in the royal gardens. But one day two emissaries from a foreign land bring a gift of a mechanical nightingale, made of gold and studded with jewels. The emperor is besotted with this shiny, clever new gift; the mechanical bird sits on a pedestal in the palace and sings all day. The real nightingale is forgotten, and slips quietly back into the forest.

But of course the emperor grows bored of the mechanical, repetitive song, and only then does he notice that his garden, once full of music, has fallen silent. He pines for the real, living nightingale and its golden singing. Until one day, when the emperor lies old, sick, and dying, the nightingale does return and sings so beautifully that death departs, and the emperor weeps and begs for the nightingale's forgiveness. The bird agrees to stay again in the garden to sing his beautiful song from dusk to dawn.

The story goes that Andersen created the tale out of love for an opera singer known as the 'Swedish nightingale'.[12] However, it could also easily be seen as an ecological fairy story, a tale about our relationship with technology and our longing for the healing beauty of nature.

One afternoon I was looking across the estuary, looking down from the stone wall outside the cottage. A few shorebirds were foraging amongst the stones and seaweed; a wagtail was hurrying about in a series of quick spurts, walking as fast as its little legs could carry it. It made a quick dart towards that stone, but then dashed back over to that clump of seaweed, seeming to forget what it was doing. Suddenly there was a commotion and everything scattered except the wagtail, which flew off for five yards, pirouetted in mid-air, and raced backwards where it had just come from. It still went to and fro, but now with much more desperation and urgency. There was a female sparrowhawk right behind it.

However quickly the small bird switched round in the air, the hawk matched its move. That hawk-mind was fixated on the small creature's flailing body; those hungry eyes were locked onto every twist in the wagtail's attempted escape flight. I was just a couple of yards above and these birds were flying directly below me. But it was so fast I could no longer tell what was happening; my eyes couldn't keep up with the sheer fear and fury of wagtail and hawk. Then, just as suddenly, the hawk dashed back into the trees and disappeared, and the wagtail also seemed to have vanished. I couldn't tell for sure what had taken place. Perhaps the sparrowhawk had caught her prey, and she would feed. But my hunch was that, although the hawk had not noticed me when she had first launched herself out of the trees, she had then become aware of my presence, had taken fright and abandoned chase, choosing instead the safety of tree cover, and allowing the wagtail to get away.

There was a shocked silence along the shoreline. Nothing moved on the beach, or stirred in the trees. Only after some minutes did quiet, uncertain voices – like cautious whispers – sound in the undergrowth, gradually becoming bolder and more confident. A few minutes later, birds were rummaging on the shoreline again. No longer was anything amiss. Life had returned to normal.

There were ravens around the estuary at Trwyn and they were magnificent flyers. Sometimes they performed such antics that you could not think of any other possible reason for it than fun, for enjoying and showing off their skills. I once watched a raven flying along when it was mobbed by a crow. The crow dived at the raven from above. The raven just flipped to one side by rolling over on its back, so that the crow missed and went sailing past.

The raven then flew three or four more wingbeats whilst still on its back, flying upside down. Finally, it did another 180-degree roll, so that it was upright again and could carry on as before. The whole manoeuvre was executed with consummate ease and lack of concern.

I also discovered that when the tide went out it exposed a natural pool that was ideal for swimming. The pool was formed out of a sandy hollow, at least a couple of metres deep and about twenty metres across. I could see fish swimming deeper down. The sun warmed the water and I swam most days: my own private swimming pool. I lay on my back floating in the salty water, feeling the buoyancy of my body increase and decrease, and my body bob up and down, as I breathed in and out. Afterwards I lay drying off in the sunshine. The last few months of my life had been busy and eventful; it was heavenly being able to relax and unwind.

This was my new style of solitary retreat: relaxed, not wilful, allowing myself to enjoy it all. Previously I would have spent that time alone reviewing and revising the last year or so, getting myself ready to re-engage back in the 'real' world. Now I felt this, here, was the real world. I hardly thought about my life back home. I forgot all about it. I just lost myself in the beautiful surroundings.

After a few days I noticed that there was a family of crows – two parents and two young – that came down to pick and scavenge on the shore. The young were short-tailed, wobble-legged, and weak-winged. One of the parents was occasionally feeding them. They followed this adult about, toddling along, looking like they might topple over at any moment.

The other parent had gone to sit on a twig of a nearby tree. Suddenly the twig gave way and the crow fell into the air. It recovered and flew to another tree, but it croaked repeatedly, as though it was annoyed, swearing in a rasping, raucous voice. Eventually the crow down on the sand gave three quieter croaks and the crow in the tree went silent, seemingly mollified.

A week later I noticed the crows again. The young had grown noticeably, especially one, which was now much bigger and more assertive than the other. It was probably the eldest. It cawed endlessly for food. It followed one or other of its parents about, screaming in a hungry, coarse, and bad-tempered voice. It leant forward, open-mouthed, and shouted for food. Then the adult bird would regurgitate food down its throat, which made a disgusting strangulated vomiting noise. The other offspring, most likely the younger, was much quieter and less demanding, and followed its parent at a further distance. I noticed that I was starting to dislike the elder sibling and I felt pleased when occasionally the younger one got a look-in.

From inside the cottage the next day I could hear the crows outside, and especially the older one, cawing for hours on end. It screamed for food pretty much non-stop. It was getting more resourceful and cunning, sometimes going to sit on a rock from where it could view each parent's movements, and flying over the moment one of them found food. It yelled, with neck thrust forward, mouth wide open. I was finding it – and its noise – rather irritating. I tried going and waving my arms about so they would fly off, but they weren't fooled for very long by my attempts at being a scarecrow. After a while they just ignored me and carried on.

It went on like this day after day. Whenever I was meditating, or sitting quietly with a cup of tea, all I could hear was the young crow shrieking. I couldn't get the noise out of my head. It was perverse: even though I found the sound unpleasant, I seemed to have got fixated on it. It was like a barb that my mind had hooked onto. Or it was like being trapped in a net, and, the more I thrashed about, annoyed and irritated, trying to get free, the more entangled I got. I cursed that crow. I even caught myself thinking I'd like to wring its neck, and cut short its monotonous bellyaching.

We speak of a flock of pigeons, or a gaggle of geese, but the collective noun for crows is 'murder'. A murder of crows: now I knew why. The way it screamed – *maw-maw-MAW-MAWRR!* – had me gritting my teeth and muttering under my breath when I was supposedly meditating.

I tried many strategies. I tried to be a good Buddhist, tried doing all the things Buddhists are supposed to do. The Buddhist in me said: 'Try contemplating that the sound, like everything, is impermanent.' 'I know the noise will stop eventually,' another voice in me replied, 'but I want it to stop *now*.'

I tried being glad of the opportunity to develop patience. I tried considering things from the point of view of the hungry young crow. I tried letting go of my attachment to how I wanted the retreat to be. The Buddha had taught a man called Bahiya that 'in the sound was only the sound': to just hear the sound itself, without labels and judgements. So I tried that too: in the 'maw' was only the 'maw'. But it sounded just as harsh and grating. I reminded myself, in the tradition of Buddhist teacher Santideva, that, although the crow was supplying the voice, I had provided the ears. I tried the practice of 'exchanging self for other' and recollected that I too was once young, dependent, and screaming for food. I tried reflecting that my enemy is my best friend because they can help teach me loving-kindness. I recalled that, according to the Tibetan tradition, the Buddhist teaching of rebirth means that all sentient beings have at one time been one's mother and this even included the young crow, and so I should feel compassion towards it. I tried to imagine what the Buddha would have done in a similar situation.

But none of it seemed to work. I was left fuming and annoyed that a *horrible* crow was making a *horrible* noise in *my* space on *my* retreat, when all I wanted was some peace and quiet.

A day or two later and the crows had grown up some more, waddling with feet wide apart, and grubbing around for their own food. But the elder sibling still kept an eye on its parents. As soon as it realized a parent had found something it reverted to 'child mode': screaming, weakly flapping its wings, running from one side of its parent to the other, then deliberately falling over and looking up still shrieking. It made itself look as helpless as possible. It was just like the way human children sometimes scream and then fall on the floor as though they've not the strength to walk. Was I anthropomorphizing the crow? Or was I seeing how much of our human behaviour is shared by animals, and originates in our animal natures?

Gradually I learnt to live with the crows and see the funny side of the situation, and, anyhow, within a few more days the young ones had grown up still further, and they were becoming less noisily demanding of their parents. But why had I been so bothered by a crow?

I thought I was living and enjoying a simple life, one of stillness and contentment. I was perhaps even a little pleased with myself for being able to live happily and easily in such a simple way. I had become rather accomplished at this business of being a hermit; it showed what a good Buddhist I was! But the fact was that I'd become rather attached to my little world. We can get attached to possessions. But we can also become attached to *not* having them. Our ego can build a little fortress of self-satisfaction around a certain style of 'simple living' – to the harmless pleasures that are freely available, to the freedom to do what we like, and to our preferred routines and habits. From the outside it might look like we are living simply, or even frugally, but actually we are living just how we like.

The real test is when we are *not* getting what we like. How does our sense of contentment and equanimity bear up then? The crow had tested me in this area. Often the beauty of nature lessens and softens our sense of self. But then something happens that we don't like, our peace is disturbed, and the ego very quickly and abruptly reasserts itself. We can take those disturbances or inconveniences personally – the crow was spoiling *my* retreat, it was too near *my* cottage. (And my crow was a pussycat compared to what nature could have thrown at me. I wasn't meditating in a jungle near the lairs of tigers. I wasn't on retreat in a snowy, icy cave in Tibet. I have a friend whose cabin was invaded by hundreds of furry caterpillars that caused an allergic reaction to her skin. I, however, only had to contend with a baby crow.)

It was both amusing and disconcerting to see how my mind, by pushing an unpleasant sensation away, actually had the effect of amplifying it and making it seem louder, closer, and more insistent. Resisting that cawing of the crow meant that my mind shrunk and contracted around the experience; it actually focused my attention on it even more strongly. It heightened the polarization in the mind between 'that thing out there' causing the unpleasant feeling, and 'poor me in here' on the receiving end of it. It made both of them – object and subject – seem more solid and substantial. My body tightened, my heart hardened, my mind locked around the experience, which meant I wanted to resist it even more.

I once heard someone tell a story about being disturbed by flies buzzing round the room while she was on retreat trying to meditate. In her mind the buzzing became louder and uglier, and increasingly dominated her meditation. She realized that, in order not to get irritated by the flies, she needed to get interested in them. Rather than meditate on the breath, or a visualized image, she meditated on sound. She listened to, and later on she watched, the flies. She learnt about their colours, their habits, their different ways of flying. Eventually she could tell by its sound what stage of life a fly was at; she could even hear when one was about to land on the window sill and die. They didn't distract her in meditation anymore.[13] The key was to listen, to listen carefully to what was actually, really going on in one's direct experience, and not to the over-amplified, distorted noise, and then the commentary on it, that one's buzzing mind was generating. Aversion exaggerates; it creates an overblown impression. But if you unclench your mind, and instead turn towards the object of aversion, then the exaggeration and disturbance subside.

The mind constantly evaluates; it can fasten onto a noise like the call of a bird and find it inherently annoying, whilst at other times it will make a different interpretation. Another friend told me about being on retreat up in the mountains when it was cold and snowy. The room in which she meditated was heated by an old wood-burning stove that would click as the metal of the stove expanded or contracted. You'd think an intermittent click could be quite irritating whilst you are trying to meditate, and one could end up tensed in anticipation of the next time it would happen. But she found her mind open, quiet, just listening. And when each click came it was sweet and blissful.

My dispute with the crow was about *control*. We want to be in control, and much of modern life is designed to maximize that control over our environment – to be able to flick a switch and produce warmth when it is cold, or cool air when it is too hot. Consumer culture conditions us into always expecting convenience and comfort. (This expectation is a huge collective delusion of course. But consumerism does come nearer than anything else in delivering convenience and comfort, which makes the delusion all the more convincing, more all-pervasive, and harder to spot.)

But when we are in nature we can't control the environment in the same way. Nature is too wild, too vast and unpredictable, and quite unconcerned with us. It doesn't care what we want. And this can be a good thing, putting us back in touch with the full texture of existence, with the plain fact that we are not king, or queen, of the universe. Life rules. It has no need to conform to our desires. The wild will not agree terms, sign a contract, or provide a guarantee or indemnity. Of course we can appreciate the comfort and convenience that modern life provides. But if our life is based solely around that comfort it ceases to seem so rich or satisfying. 'Control', in the sense I am talking about, can be dulling, deadening. To find the real treasure there has to be an element of the raw and the risky.

One of the potential dangers of solitude is that we might get into this attitude of 'control'. This can happen on a solitary retreat, or, perhaps even more so, if living on our own in an urban environment. In today's society an increasing number of people live on their own. Is there a danger that this can become overly individualistic, that we end up putting more and more energy into building cosy little lives that are all about *my* comfort, *my* likes and dislikes? After my time at Waingap, after many years of living in communities, I lived on my own for a couple of years, and it was at a time when my working life was also mostly solitary. In the end I decided that, for me, it wasn't that healthy. I noticed my mind more and more preoccupied and ruminating about what I wanted to eat, or read, or do. I circled round in a small, self-enclosed world. Minor inconveniences (the cawing of a crow) could then loom larger than life; they took up a disproportionate amount of time and energy. We need elements in our lives that are *not* about us, that draw us out of a subjectivity that is ultimately limiting and painful. (I am quite prepared to accept, however, that other people may have a different experience from me. For example, it has been pointed out that a striking number of writers, artists, and philosophers have lived predominantly solitary lives, but ones that were happy and richly creative. Nor does living alone preclude having loving and meaningful relationships.[14])

Henry Thoreau wrote:

To be awake is to be alive. I have never yet met a man who was quite awake. How could I have looked him in the face?[15]

I wonder if Thoreau was aware that the word 'Buddha' means 'one who is awake'. How can we live so that we will be really awake, or at least more fully so? I can think of three types of situation in my life when I feel at my most alive and awake. And, in all of them, there is a connection between this 'aliveness' and my attitude to 'control'.

One is at certain times when I've been part of a collective project that has drawn on the abilities and goodwill of a number of people, including myself, and when we are working at full stretch, at the edge of our personal capacities, really giving of ourselves in order to create or achieve something that we deeply believe in. The situation may be big and challenging, not just out of my control, but beyond the control of any, or all, of us. Yet I am sure that, whatever happens, we will respond well and find a way through. These kinds of situations can draw us out of ourselves; we can give more than we thought we had, and afterwards we realize that for a lot of the time we were hardly thinking about ourselves, rarely anxious or irritable. We were at our very best, and this was deeply satisfying. The experience comes with an unfamiliar and striking combination of two qualities that might at first seem opposed to each other: confidence and humility. In those situations I can feel engaged and effective, more than usually confident. I feel my own potency. And yet at the same time I know and really feel that the project is much bigger than me, that I could never pull it off on my own, and that I am totally dependent on the skills, energy, and perspectives of others.

The second type of situation is when I've been helping to care for someone who is seriously ill and dying. On these occasions, living more fully in the presence of death, I can feel strangely, intensely alive, more in touch with the preciousness of life. This, too, can cause me to drop so many of my usual, relatively trivial, worries and concerns. What is going on is just too big, too deep, way beyond anyone's control and so, in my better moments, I let go of that control and simply respond as best I can to the needs of the situation. Again, these kinds of situations can draw more out of me than I knew I had, and bring forth qualities of generosity and patience. And it is utterly real: I am in touch with both the gloss and the grit of life. It can be surprising, however, how quickly this awareness fades away once life returns to 'normal'. It is hard to stay alive and awake, hard to keep looking life so fully in the face.

The third situation when I can often feel more truly alive and awake is when I'm immersed and alone in nature. This aliveness doesn't necessarily or automatically happen. I have needed to learn how to make the most of the opportunity offered by the wild. I can still sometimes crave experiences in nature, in a way that actually limits and makes shallow. Or, at other times, I can really *be* in nature, and be receptive to what it can teach. My attitude to the crow in Trwyn was unreal, deluded. I was being driven, unconsciously, by a myth of perfection and desire for control. But, at other times, nature wakes me up, rouses me into fuller life. My senses become more nuanced and vivid, a deeper awareness is stimulated. Nature's riches and beauty help me to be more content. The heart can open more fully and the world comes flooding in. The trick I've learnt is to not then get attached to the pleasure, not close down into an attitude of control, but to stay open to the full range of experience. True contentment is beyond even pleasure and pain. Then, this more vivid aliveness to the world means there is a quietening of the self, a lessening of the ego. Because there is more world, there is less self. And because there is less self, there is even more world – saturated with life and aliveness.

6

A night on Hawk Hill

Every once in a while, usually whilst I am doing a solitary retreat, I pack my army surplus bivouac bag and head out for the night. I've slept up mountains, in hedgerows, along old, disused railway lines, and on cliff tops. I only do this occasionally, mostly in the summer, and when I think the weather will be good: I'm not as hardened as some outdoor types! But I've long relished the chance to roam out further, not needing to get back that night to the place where I'm staying. Each time I love the sense of freedom and adventure, and encountering the different atmospheres of the dusk, the night, and the dawn.

Whilst still at Trwyn, the old ferryman's cottage at the mouth of the estuary, I headed for the hills to spend the night on nearby Hawk Hill. The day before I had felt excited planning this trip, but then, on the day itself, I shilly-shallied. I came up against resistance, knowing that probably a fairly sleepless, uncomfortable night awaited me. I hesitated, wondering if it could go wrong, or if the weather might turn foul. Or I worried that I had not packed enough food to keep me going, so I prepared some more. Then I was anxious that I had too much food and that it would go bad and be wasted. I dithered out of an underlying desire to keep things cosy and comfortable.

There was also an element of fear. Quite a lot of the fear wasn't about the dark, or of the wild, or wild animals, or even fear of the pain and nuisance of midge bites or cold, wet weather. It was fear of humans. I feared that I was doing something 'wrong', eccentric, or mildly subversive, and that I might meet someone who could be disapproving, and maybe they would even phone the police and have me moved on.

One time previously it was getting dark, and I was just settling down on the edge of some woodland for the night, when I heard the sound of a motorized vehicle. I hid in the undergrowth, peered out through the stalks of hogweed as best I could, and tried to keep my head down. Two men came along on a quad bike. They were wearing rather odd-looking, and identical, black helmets and uniforms. They seemed to have quite serious and intent expressions on their faces, though it was hard to see in the gloom and through all the greenery. They looked so strange that I wondered if I'd accidentally wandered onto the set of a low-budget television science-fiction series, or whether it was some kind of night-time paintballing outfit. Or maybe they were just gamekeepers from the local estate going to check on something. They were coming in my direction. I was convinced that the vehicle headlights were shining right at me. They were sure to see me. Perhaps they had already spotted me from afar and were coming to sort me out, thinking I was a poacher. I imagined them catching me and looking sceptical when I swore I was vegetarian. They got within a couple of yards of me, and then carried on past into the woods. I lay back down in my sleeping bag, trying to listen out for sounds above the drumming of my own heart.

But, on this occasion at Trwyn, it was a beautiful clear-blue midsummer day and the prospects looked ideal. I fantasized that later that evening I'd be lying on my back in the grass looking up at the stars, and the following morning waking to the glorious sunrise. At last, then, as soon as the tide was low enough, I stepped out across the saltmarsh and the many textures of sand. The tide having only just turned, much of the sand was still watery and sloppy, like a wet mix of cement. In some places it was soft and mushy, like a foam mattress, which was much more demanding on the leg muscles. Other times it was hard, compact, and ridged, like a rucked-up rubber mat.

Next I was walking across meadowlands full of wildflowers, meadow pipits, and skylarks singing. Two hares saw me coming and moved into the longer grass, pressing their hips down onto the ground, and flattening their ears back. The colours of the grasses and their seed heads were the most beautiful thing, earthy but glowing. I tried to name or describe the colours, but it was very difficult. The colours were elusive, like a faint scent on a breeze. They weren't single tones, but complex chords and harmonies of colour, a mingling and mixing of hues, soft and subtle, whilst also full of richness and resonance. I gave them names like 'rosy-wheat-fen', 'burgundy-honey', 'rusting-apple-green', 'pink-brindled-fawn', 'burnished-claret', or 'lilac-kissed-copper'.

I started to climb upwards and the land got harder and more muscly. The vegetation changed also; there were unfurling bracken, foxgloves, and heather whose colour was just one or two tones darker pink than the foxgloves. I clambered over a lichen-covered stone wall, higher still, and the ground became boggy and mossy. I noticed the yellow stars, with their orange tips, of bog-asphodel flowers, as well as sundew plants, butterwort, spotted orchid, and the tiny yellow flowers of tormentil. Bilberry was the brightest; the leaves had a spring-like shine in the sun, they glowed with green.

The path up was steep and heavy-going, especially as I was carrying a rucksack with sleeping bag, food, and a couple of litres of water. I was sweating so much that my glasses kept sliding down my nose. The excited anticipation of adventure had diminished; it had become a slog and I needed to focus all my energy.

The weather had been gradually changing too. It had become hazy, then thin cloud had begun forming in the distance, then whiter, wispier cloud blew up behind me and over the hill. It got much cooler, though sometimes it cleared and there, for a few moments, were the sun and blue sky again. The cloud raced fast over my head when the wind got up. It was eerie being enfolded within this cloud that flared bright white with the sunlight. The cloud captured the light and held it; even though I could no longer directly see the sun, the cloud glared brilliantly. By early evening I was up on the top. The mountain fell away dramatically on the other side, a chasm of slate-grey and Mars-red rock. Luckily, beneath the cloud, I could still see the view: green forestry plantations below and the Snowdon range of mountains on the other side of the valley. Probably Snowdon had been busy with people that day, but here, just a few miles away, I hadn't met anyone at all.

I found a sheltered spot, or so I thought, behind a drystone wall. However, the wind was rushing through the gaps; it was not only cold, but noisy too. To keep warm, I unrolled my sleeping bag and cocooned myself inside. There was nothing else to do, except look and listen. I sat and watched the clouds and the sun lowering in the sky. The shadows were lengthening, distorting the shapes and forms in the rock, subduing the colours, and darkening the atmosphere. There was an eerie contrast in that above and around me the cloud rushed by, but in the distance it danced in slow motion. It was like watching two films simultaneously, one speeded up, and the other slowed down. Nearby, the wind was a constant blast that shoved and hurried the cloud along. In the distance the clouds were more flowing, bobbing, and playful, like astronauts doing t'ai chi.

Gradually the mountains turned into silhouettes, the colours faded to grainy darkness. I had found a different place to sleep, a sheltered ledge, and I went there now. I was warm enough wrapped up in my sleeping bag, though the ground was lumpy. A small bird flew past, or rather was blown over my head. Now that it was dark, large slugs were coming out from hiding places, shiny and black, like thick curls of liquorice. I shuddered at the thought of one creeping into my ear in the night-time. There was to be no stargazing that night. For a while I could just make out the moon through the cloud. It was a weird sodium-orange, then it turned buttery-yellow, then nothing at all was visible through the rushing grey.

I awoke as it started getting light again at 4am, a gradual paling of the dark grey. There was a white-out, a misty cloud that meant I could only see about twenty yards ahead at the most. I was disappointed, demotivated. I lay there waiting to see if it would blow or burn off, but nothing shifted. My plan had been to spend the day exploring further, but the desire had gone. My body was stiff, my legs surprisingly wobbly, and I could hardly see what was around me. Demoralized, I decided to get up and simply make my way back down again. I returned by the most direct route that took me past craggy rocks, old mine shafts, and then rough and scraggy ground where no paths were marked. I was dispirited, just trudging downwards, waiting to get home.

I was coming down from the mountain, coming steep down through a bomb blast of rock and scree. The hillside was shattered. For uncountable numbers of years it had been battered by the elements, scoured by ice, scourged with wind. It was a landslide of shards, heaped up into deep trench-like burrows and hollows, a place that I could easily imagine as savage and hostile in the winter. It was like clambering through the rubbled ruins of an old village. In my imagination I could make out the remains of an old dwelling here, or a wall along there – the remnants of what was now just a ghost town. A wheatear was flustering from one rocky perch to another, scolding, breathless with panic. A few weak rays of sunlight angled through the cloud, slanting down into the rocks, accentuating the gaps and crevices, deepening the darkness. In those cave-like shadows down below me I thought I saw young foxes playing, but when I looked again I could see nothing.

Suddenly I did definitely see a fox, an adult, climbing over a boulder. I stopped and watched, and when it got over the boulder the fox saw me too, and stopped and considered me. I had not met or interacted with a human being for weeks. I had just spent the night alone on a cloud-shrouded mountain. And now a fox and I looked intently at each other.

We were on the same level, not much more than ten yards apart, gazing at one another. The fox seemed different from the urban foxes with which I am familiar. Its coat was thick; the hair round its ears and on the back of its head was especially long and straggly, wild looking, like the mane of a wild horse. The sunshine filled the fur round its ears, blazed orange-red and made the fox seem bigger. But the creature's gaze, the steady look in its black eyes, was even more compelling. It didn't look questioning, or afraid, or uncertain, or wondering-what-to-do. The fox just held my gaze, watching and waiting. It stood its ground. I could tell that the fox belonged in that place. This was a creature of the mountains. That look was a look from the wild.

I was taken by surprise, but the fox seemed as steady as the mountain, patient as granite. We had been standing there for only a few seconds, but it felt like much longer. The fox's gaze was a long look from out of time, or at least out of the time created by the ticking of the human mind. In my own mind, that internal ticking was getting faster and louder: 'Wow! It's a mountain fox! I wonder if it will move? How long have we been standing here?' I am not saying I wanted to be like the fox; I was on my way back to the comfort of my cottage, hot food and drink. Later on I would be able to remember and ponder on 'my' fox. I would be able to tell my friends about him, share the experience with others.

Still, that fox taught me something about being alive. It had a different style of consciousness, another way of being, that reflected and relativized my own human mode of functioning. That look: that unremitting gaze threw me back on myself, heightened my human self-consciousness. The fox made me more aware of being a human being, standing there, perhaps slightly clumsily on all those boulders and rocks, in that strange place. Its awareness was bang on in the now, and smack on in the senses, whereas mine was a mind that would wander out of the world and lose itself in an interior talking space. The same human mind that could later wonder at the experience was also the mind that, in the moment, could distract and dilute by grasping at the experience, through wanting to 'have' an experience. I couldn't just *be* in the experience; I had to keep telling myself I was *having* the experience, which then partially removed me from it. Human self-awareness sometimes sharpens, sometimes makes blunt. The human mind is a knife brought to a whetstone, held either graspingly, clumsily, forcefully, or with skill and lightness of touch. This attitude we bring to our awareness is a choice we are making every moment of our waking lives.

I also felt slightly afraid. At the same time, I felt foolish for feeling afraid. I knew rationally that it was only a fox. It wasn't really dangerous, like meeting a bear in the wilderness, or a tiger in the jungle. Perhaps the fox was more frightened of me, although it didn't look fearful. But to be standing there in that strange dark place, not having spoken to another human for days, all alone with a fox. On some level of my being there was fear. It was mingled with other contradictory emotions. I found the fox beautiful; I was delighted to meet it, felt almost a love for it. I felt strangely blessed by our meeting. I was also aware that behind this adult fox there were young cubs hidden away in the rocks, and I wanted to respect their space and not disturb or frighten any of them.

For what seemed like a long time, that creature and I gazed at each other, unblinking. Eventually, rather awkwardly, I looked down at my feet, to check my footing on the uneven rocks, and to begin to walk away. A second later I looked up again. The fox was gone. I saw no move, no blur of red. The fox had disappeared.

I moved off to the right, circling round where I thought the family of foxes might be, and all the while looking backwards, hoping for another glimpse of them. As I carried on down the hill, I wondered about that underlying fear. Why had I felt afraid? Was it being alone in that unknown place, a strange place with a strong atmosphere? In meeting a wild animal, was some deep-buried, almost forgotten, instinct reactivated? Maybe the incident triggered a natural, inborn impulse that dated back to my own wild human ancestry and origins?

But perhaps there is also something about being human that alienates us from nature and that also creates fear. D.H. Lawrence's famous poem 'Snake' describes the writer coming out of his dwelling to get water, only to find a snake is drinking from his trough. He watches, fascinated and entranced by the snake. Yet he also knows from the colour of its skin that it is poisonous and that some people in his situation would want the snake killed. And he feels fear, and then is embarrassed for feeling fear, wondering what others might think if they saw him there waiting for a snake to finish drinking. His human pride is bitten. He doesn't want a mere snake to get the better of him. So when the snake slowly turns to go, he lashes out at it, by throwing a log in its direction.

And immediately he regrets it:

For he seemed to me again like a king,
Like a king in exile, uncrowned in the underworld,
Now due to be crowned again.

And so, I missed my chance with one of the lords of life.
And I have something to expiate;
A pettiness.[16]

I knew what had happened to Lawrence, I felt what he felt: that fear, then, through pride, being embarrassed to feel fear, even though there were no humans around to be embarrassed in front of!

We human beings have evolved and developed *self*-consciousness. We don't just have *sense*-consciousness; we can also be aware of having sense experience, we can be aware of being aware. This enables us to 'stand back' from our experience, to observe and reflect. And this allows us to understand our environment, to form ideas and theories about how it works, and then to be able to control and manipulate that environment to our own advantage. Out of this arises the whole human world, from the first primitive tools and artefacts, through to our modern world of science, culture, and astonishing human ingenuity, creativity, and sophistication.

This has huge advantages in terms of the human ability to adapt the physical world to meet our needs and desires. But there is a price. That human faculty of standing back, reflecting, and understanding, and then envisaging how things could be different, also means that humans are frequently restless and anxious. However much we have, we can imagine having *more*, or things being *better*. However well things are going, we can imagine circumstances in which they might not go so well, meaning we forfeit what we've earnt.

Imagination has given man flexibility; but in doing so, has robbed him of contentment.[17]

The very evolution of consciousness that allows for such supreme adaptability and creativity also creates human unease, a sense of perpetual worry. Perhaps it is this anxiety that spurs humans on to new feats of productivity and creativity; there is a cyclic relationship at work.

We are animals, our creaturely nature presses upon us – the urge to survive, to thrive, to reproduce, and to fear whatever, or whoever, is perceived to threaten our security. These basic drives work on, and through, our distinctively human self-consciousness. We are hunter-gatherers whose instinct is to accumulate, to grab opportunity when it arises. Our senses are evolved and adapted to newness and novelty, keeping us alert to any opportunity that might be exploited. Even once we've achieved comfort and security, our instinct is to carry on, to look for more, in case we lose what we've got.

Human self-consciousness is a double-edged sword. It allows us to stand back, observe, understand, and control the world. Yet, in doing so, it also creates that particularly human sense of dissatisfaction, that underlying, nagging feeling that we've never arrived, never finished, that, no matter how busy we are or how much we get done, our life is never completed.

Because of that self-consciousness we also have a sense of being individual and therefore being separate. We are social creatures who instinctively want to stand out from the group and be noticed, whilst at the same time we want to fit in and belong. Out of all these competing drives and desires arises the human tendency to compare ourselves with others. We measure ourselves up against each other, judging whether we are better or worse. This is the human emotion of pride. We don't want anyone or anything getting one over on us, and this creates an underlying anxiety and fear of potential humiliation. We want to be in control and, moreover, we want to be *seen* to be in control. This pride cuts us off from other humans and from the non-human world also. The human state is one of subtle loneliness and alienation, even though we may not usually notice it. It was that sense of separateness that I had touched into on the mountainside.

This is the human condition. Later on, thinking back to that night alone on the mountain and the morning encounter with the fox, I wondered about the possibility of overcoming that human condition. I thought about another encounter with a snake – that of the Buddha. The stories of the time immediately after the Buddha's enlightenment describe him staying for several weeks in the same spot, by a group of trees near the Niranjana River. Through those weeks he lived and meditated under a number of different trees, and in each place there was a further unfolding of his enlightenment experience. Then there was a huge and unseasonable storm, the daytime going dark, the sky thrashing with monsoon-like rains, and deep, heavy thunder. A huge cobra-like snake came out of the undergrowth and coiled its body around the meditating Buddha, and held its head over him, so that the Buddha was totally protected from the storm.[18]

The story comes from a very different time and culture from that of the modern West, and its mythic imagery may seem strange and fantastical. The snake could be said to symbolize all our coiled-up psychic energy, our dragon-like wildness, which in the Buddha had been fully released, flowing in perfect harmony with the good, fully integrated into his experience of enlightenment. But it can also be seen as a symbol of the Buddha's complete harmony with nature around him. He had overcome that human alienation. The Buddha had evolved beyond human self-awareness. He knew that subject and object aren't really separate, but arise together – and that to identify and grasp hold of 'me' (through pride) and 'mine' (through restless craving) is a delusion. He wasn't over-identified with the subjective side of that polarization. It is from that sense of a separate 'me' that comparison and pride arise. The Buddha had overcome that human isolation.[19]

By the afternoon, when I had made my way back down from Hawk Hill and was returning across the estuary, the weather was sunny. My spirits had picked up again. I was glad I'd been up there, in that strange atmosphere and light. I was glad I'd had that surprise meeting with the fox. I hadn't been stargazing or watching the sunrise as I'd been expecting or hoping. Once again, however, the wildness of a place and its creatures had spoken to me, teaching me something about the nature of my mind, and about being human.

7

Solitary together

Six years ago, aged 89, after a year's illness, my father died. Until that last year he had enjoyed good health and had a happy retirement. Into his late eighties he still rode about town on his pushbike and swam at least once every week in the local swimming pool. I could easily have imagined him active into his nineties. But then his energy waned, his health deteriorated, and eventually tests revealed that he had stomach cancer. He was told there was no treatment, which he accepted with characteristic stoicism. He was uncomplaining and unfussy.

Fortunately for me, my job at this time wasn't tied to an office or specific location, and I could do it almost anywhere. This meant I could move down and stay near my parents, spend more time with my father in his last days, keep my brother updated on the situation, and do what I could to help and support my mother. For those few weeks in January and February of that year I visited him every day in the hospital, reminisced with him about his life, watched football on TV with him, or read him stories from his favourite book (a poignant reminder of how he had once read bedtime stories to me). Joy and pain were woven fine; opposite emotions were strangely and unfamiliarly intertwined. Our hearts were light with love and tenderness. Our hearts were heavy with sadness and helplessness. As his illness progressed he grew weaker and more confused, but this manifested as an almost child-like sweetness. At the end, his mild and gentle good nature was what shone through. Just a few days before he died, now in the advanced stages of cancer, he told me he had woken up that morning completely happy.

A few weeks after his death, I took myself away for a fortnight. Perhaps this seems a strange time to choose solitude? Didn't I want to be with others in my – and their – time of grief? I had helped my mother arrange the funeral and do the practical and administrative things that needed to be done. She had shown no hint of self-pity, talked about the future in a positive fashion, and seemed to be dealing with her bereavement remarkably well. I felt confident that my mother would cope. Maybe it was even necessary for her to be in the flat on her own now, and for her to enter another phase of coming to terms with her loss. Usually I would not phone or contact anyone whilst on a solitary retreat; this time, however, I made an exception and checked in with my mother a few times. But, apart from this, I wanted to spend the time alone.

I stayed for the fortnight in a small, comfortable dwelling on an organic farm in Dorset. The place was let out as an artist's studio, although the owners were also used to people doing solitary retreats there. They appreciated and welcomed people being on retreat and meditating there, and told me that they thought it had a beneficial effect on the land. The little dwelling looked across a field to the biscuit-brown ridge of shingle that was Chesil Beach, less than a five-minute walk away. On a clear day it looked as if I could reach my arm out the window and scoop up a handful of sea. On a cloudy day it seemed as if the sea was far out of reach, even miles away.

A slanted tree along the shoreline leant with the fierce wind whilst also straining for sunlight; its situation and circumstance forced uniqueness and distinctiveness, beauty in adversity, a strange and twisted grace – wind made visible. The shingle stretched as far as the eye could see in either direction, and all along it grew plants that were adapted to the windy, salty conditions: plants that kept low out of the wind and crept along the ground, plants with special waxy leaves that wouldn't dehydrate, plants with roots that ran for metres underground seeking out the moisture and nutriment. Here, as everywhere, nature was supremely adaptable, opportunistic; it was life springing up wherever, whenever, however the prevailing conditions would allow.

The size of the shingle gradually increases as one travels from west to east along the coastline. Around West Bexington the gravelly stones are no more than pea-sized; a few miles further east they become as big as a broad bean; by the time you reach the Fleet each stone is about the size of a small potato. Legend has it that in times past smugglers coming ashore in the dark of night could judge where they had landed by reaching down for a handful of pebbles. The earth and the moon, and the sea and the wind, have, for countless years, been rounding out those pebbles, and sorting them by size, continually and gradually altering the shapes and contours of the landscape.

The beach near where I was staying is formed of a series of steps, or steep banks, where the shingle suddenly drops away for a metre or two. I observed how the shape of the shore worked with the waves. Sometimes a wave would thump up against the vertical face of a step, throwing shingle into the air. Other times the wave would come over the ledge, and then there would be a huge hissing, sucking, and sizzling as seawater drew back through the gaps between the stones. Since the shingle was so fine and small, the gaps were numerous and intricate, and this created an especially loud hiss. It was a pristine hiss, long and gasping, a roaring hiss that rushed right inside the cavities of my ears and brain, cleansing, rinsing, purifying.

The steep banked shape of the shoreline also meant that, if I stood on the next ledge up, I'd be only a couple of yards from the waves breaking loud and big just below me. It was quite different from being on a sandy beach with a smoother gradient on which the waves broke far out and then washed in to shore. The waves on Chesil Beach were sudden crashers, rather than long rollers. The air was full of spray and salty mist. The salt and swash of the sea got right into my eyes, ears, nose, mouth, lungs, deep into the pores of my skin and the roots of my hair.

As Thomas A. Clark wrote in his short poem 'Five waves':

to learn to look at the sea is to learn to look
to learn to listen to the sea is to learn to listen[20]

I spent hours trudging along the shingle, staring out to sea, listening to the waves, and breathing deep of the cleansing, bracing, briny air. It was a good place to be right then. I was, of course, vividly aware of my father, though with a much more consistent awareness than I would have been able to sustain back in my usual busy circumstances. My mother had lent me a collection of photos of him from different phases of his life, and I pinned these up all over the walls in the studio. I had the time and the inner space to keep him in mind constantly, to think of him and his life fully and deeply, to recall and remember especially the last months of his life, and to record in my journal some of the things he had said before they slipped from my memory. Every time I closed my eyes to meditate I saw him and his smiling face looking up from the hospital bed, and several times he appeared in my dreams.

Emotions surged back and forth like the tide. One day I saw a boat offshore that I knew he would have found interesting, and I imagined myself telling him about it later on. Then there came the pang of realization that this wasn't possible. Recollecting what he had told me of his life, I would think of questions to put to him. Then there came the shock of remembering I couldn't ask him anything ever again. Sometimes I found myself laughing at something he had said in the hospital. Sometimes I felt regret: there had been one or two occasions where he had suddenly said something significant, and to which, in my surprise, I hadn't responded as well as I would have liked. Perhaps I had missed an opening, an opportunity for communication? What might have transpired if I could have had more presence of mind? Again, I would never know. Sometimes I wondered if I should have expressed love and gratitude more explicitly more often than I did, although I also knew that he was a quiet, reserved man who didn't like overt displays of emotion. My grief felt closely related to gratitude, to my knowing just how deeply I was indebted to my father, and the realization that I could never repay him. I didn't know what to do with that massive debt; it was like a gaping hole inside me. It took me a long time to understand that I didn't need to do anything with it, except to remember.

The waves of grief swelled and broke inside my heart, but I never felt overcome by them. I felt surprisingly uplifted, though it was a calm, quiet, and sober inspiration. My father had died peacefully and well. Right at the end of his life he taught me something very precious. I thought I had been there to help him, but I had been humbled by what he had shown me about how to die. Being with him as he passed away made death more real and immediate, but also less frightening and unknown. Perhaps I would now know how to die, when my time came. This was the last gift he gave me.

It was late March, and the swallows arrived suddenly, catching flies above and around a pond in the field on the way down to the sea. For a long time they swirled at high velocity, stocking up on food after their long journey. But, however fast they hurtled, they flicked aside instantly if they came close to colliding. As they passed by, they chirped at one another. To my ears it sounded rather nonchalant, quite unlike the excited screaming of swifts.

There was no doubt that spring was arriving. The marsh of another nearby field reverberated with what sounded like gurgling drainpipes. Frogs were breeding. Although I could clearly hear this chorus of belches, it was very hard to catch sight of them; each frog sensed my footsteps and all I would see was a leaping body, a splash, and it was gone, reminding me of Basho's famous haiku:

The old pond –
a frog jumps in,
sound of water.[21]

Two shelducks hurried along, following the shoreline, and I also saw three pintail ducks. Half a mile on and there was the sound of a skylark filling the whole field. I looked upwards, screwing up my eyes to see where it was. Where was all that rich, clear sound coming from? Eventually I could make out a speck against the cloud, just about spy its wings whirring. The song cascaded down like a silver stream. The lark sang fast, breathlessly. It was like an evangelist in ecstasy, fervently praying, pouring out his heart, so brimming with faith that the words flowed unbrokenly. Then the lark plummeted to ground and the field fell silent again.

Walking uphill and inland, I discovered a landscape of long, gradual chalk and limestone hills, the earth yellow, bronzy, and full of flints, a land of gorse heathland and green farmland, and also a land of prehistoric ridgeways, burial sites, and stone circles. I could feel the centuries, the millennia, how the land had been lived and worked on for thousands of years. It was archetypally England; it felt ancient, but somehow familiar, intimate, and homely. The land was like a well-weathered stone, its rough edges smoothed, its surfaces softened and embroidered with lichen. I sensed that the pathways I walked were similarly ancient, the old ways by which, long ago, pedlars travelled, and villagers went to seek work on fields and farms.

Along the beach on most days, especially at weekends, was a long line of fishermen, siting themselves about twenty yards apart, stretching as far as the eye could see. Sometimes, to provide a bit of warmth, they made little bonfires out of driftwood and the numerous cuttlefish bones that were scattered along the shore. The fishermen caught mackerel and tossed them onto the beach behind them. To prevent the mackerel flapping back into the sea, they would throw them into a bowl-shaped cavity they'd sculpted out in the shingle with their hands. The fish would thrash about, in a fit of terror, as if the shingle was electrified and contact with it gave the poor creature a terrible shock. The fisherman would have turned his back, facing back to the sea, attending to his rod, so he wouldn't notice all this going on behind him. Perhaps he didn't want to see. The terrible, urgent thrashing would get weaker after a minute or two, there would be pauses, then longer more exhausted pauses, then hardly any movement at all, just feeble twitching, and then stillness.

I watched the flashing white wings of a tern, and its black watching eye, and the way it folded its body and fell into the water, slicker than quicksilver, coming up with a fish, a tiny sliver of silver in its orange bill. The bird's hover and dive was so graceful, the streamlined shape so elegant: the pressure to survive, the sheer urge of life to live, creates a kind of perfection. In our contingent, conditioned world there is both suffering and beauty. The truth of one does not negate the truth of the other. In fact, beauty is sometimes our astonishment at the striving of life, a striving that takes a creature to the edge of physical possibility. 'Beauty is not adventitious, but essential', as Nan Shepherd once put it.[22]

I felt so fortunate to have those two weeks, to have time to think of my father undistractedly, and to absorb and come to terms with the fact that he had gone. All this was in keeping with my experience of other periods of solitude. On those, I would often experience aloneness, but also feel strongly connected with the other people in my life. This might seem paradoxical, but often in solitude what is truly important and meaningful rises to the surface of awareness. I know, and I feel, what really matters. And, most of all, what really matters is our connection with others.

Even when alone we are in relationship; who we are is so dependent on others. On this occasion, for example, I was vividly conscious of my father's influence in my life, of the qualities, traits, views I had learnt, imbibed, inherited from him. In a way, all this is obvious, but when alone we have the inner space to realize it and feel it more fully. Times of solitude have helped me to savour and appreciate both my aloneness and my connection. I have this sense of 'me' floating around inside my head: in our very subjectivity there is a fundamental aloneness and separation. And yet we are influencing one another all the time: our actions, words, or thoughts eddy outwards, creating currents that rock or lull those around us, precipitating them into sending out more waves that merge or rebound with ours into complex rippling patterns. We are fundamentally connected.

Sometimes our modern lives can be so hectic and busy that we don't have time to *really* think about people, to consider them beyond the everyday practicalities of living and getting on. Often it is when I am away on my own that I become more strongly conscious of my friends and family. They can feel surprisingly present and close. I come back from my time away with a renewed and reinvigorated heart connection with them. I return home with a fuller appreciation of a particular person, or a stronger sense of how I could be a better friend to someone else, or a clearer understanding and sympathy towards another person whose actions had previously seemed so baffling and infuriating.

Sometimes people ask if going on retreat isn't rather escapist, or selfish. Or is solitude for people who are loners, or for the socially inadequate?! Those who have tasted solitude know there is nothing escapist about it. Quite the opposite: when alone you have no choice but to face your moods, thoughts, whims. You can no longer blame anyone else for them. Being alone is a long look into the mirror of the mind. It is much harder to ignore that mirror than when back in the midst of a busy life surrounded by opportunities for distraction. Nor is going away to be quiet and alone necessarily selfish: my motive for going is partly to return to my ordinary life with more to give. And, although I am by character shy and introverted, I don't go on solitary retreats to escape from people, or because I'm unhappy. It might seem paradoxical, but being alone can strengthen your connection with others.

My mother had given me a box containing letters to and from my father that he had filed away, and various press cuttings and photocopied articles that he had collected. On that first retreat, just after he died, it felt too soon to look into the material. I had enough to take in and assimilate already. But later that year I got the chance to spend another week quietly, and I devoted it to investigating the contents of my 'father's box'.

The week coincided with the winter solstice and I stayed in a caravan in Denbighshire, in North Wales. It had a big window that looked out over the fields and hills. The far hills were still snow-covered, but elsewhere the snow was melting away and it was noticeably milder. I felt happy to be there and relaxed into the familiar feeling of retreat, the sense of space and time opening out. I enjoyed watching the ravens chasing each other in big circles, wheeling and diving. Treecreepers often visited the ash trees outside the caravan, and a nuthatch pickaxed at the trunks too. There was the scream of jays, and a pheasant with a mechanical croak that gradually speeded up, like a rusty old motor engine being cranked up and eventually kicking into gear.

Mossy greens, spiky blacks, and deadpan greys: the palette of colours in the fields, hedges, and sky was subtle and beautiful, despite the dullness of the day. Fungus the colour of marigold was bursting out of the rough wizened stems of a gorse bush. The hedges were all hacked at with farm machinery, twigs and debris were scattered all over the lane. Meltwater sloshed across fields into streams and drains, leaving piles of sodden leaves slumped up in the gutter. The land was muddy and messy, and it smelt cold and damp. This was weather for turning in.

I had a whole week to discover and explore the contents of my father's box. I was surprised how much was in there and how well ordered it was, arranged into different categories, each in its own envelope. (It made me rather ashamed that I had mislaid so many of the letters sent to me over the years.) I spent several hours each day slowly sifting through the box, and reading a large proportion of its contents. As the days went by, I delved deeper into the box, which meant reaching further back in time. The letters from my father were written in careful and beautiful handwriting and were almost completely free of errors or crossings out; he had been a primary-school teacher and had impeccably neat and tidy joined-up writing. There were letters to and from my brother and me, when we were both in our late teens and early twenties, just leaving home and breaking away from aspects of our upbringing. Some of the letters from the two of us were very forthright, written with the pure intensity of youth, and, reading them now, I wondered what it had been like for him to receive them.

There were passionately argued letters he had written during the 1970s, when he was in his mid-forties, and when he had become convinced that Christianity, and its injunction to love your neighbour as yourself, implied socialism and equality. He came from a devout, old-fashioned, working-class Catholic family who would have been more traditional and conservative in their views, and I wondered what had caused him to change his attitudes at this time of his life. Sadly, I would never be able to ask him. Near the bottom of the pile was a whole series of letters to him from his own father, written during the Second World War. I never knew my grandfather; he died before I was born. Reading these letters I could picture a very devout, strict, though not unkind, hardworking man, terribly serious about Catholicism and religion. 'The war has happened because God has allowed it,' he wrote, 'and we must therefore accept it and see it as a punishment for man's wicked ways.'

There were lots of gaps. For example, there were no copies of letters from my father before the 1970s, only letters written to him. But, even so, I caught glimpses of my father as a younger man, younger than I had known him. I got flashes of the passion and intensity of his younger self. I was left wondering, and there were many questions I would have loved to have asked him. Reading the contents of the box I felt I understood more of him and his conditioning – childhood in the Catholic Church in the first half of the twentieth century and, later, the hopes and doubts triggered by the reform and liberalization of the Second Vatican Council. All that meant I could also understand more about the forces and conditions that, a generation later, had shaped and influenced me. It was a deeply stirring experience and I felt so glad it happened in this spacious and open way, in circumstances where I had time to more fully absorb and reflect. I could allow the contents of the letters to sink into my imagination much more deeply, to try and feel what he might have felt and experienced.

I felt so fortunate I had been able to spend time in these places, first along the shingly, salt-sprayed, crashing shoreline, and then up on these snow-washed wintry hills. Held by these spaces, I could really see and hear, feel and understand something of my father, and, through him, something of myself. As I had noticed during previous times of solitude, I saw once more how the heart needs time, needs space to fully open out. Then we can more fully realize our connection with others, more fully feel our indebtedness to them.

8

'World is crazier and more of it than we think'

As there was no visible path, I chose the most accessible-looking part of the hillside and zigzagged my way up. Once I reached the ridge, the terrain was easier going: grassy, mossy, peaty black earth. There was a dark tarn full of tadpoles and water beetles. A golden plover, in its beautiful summer plumage, circled round me and called out. I followed the ridge upwards. It became suddenly much rockier, a strange, stark, stripped-naked landscape of bare grey rock that appeared to have been pushed up in great rough heaps, or thrown down the steep mountainside. The ridge undulated and sometimes I couldn't see further than about ten yards ahead. It looked like it just petered out. But if I persevered, and followed where the map indicated, then the way forward became apparent.

According to my map, the hill I was climbing was called Sgurr na Ba Glaise. To me, right then, this sounded beautiful and evocative. When I looked up the words in a Gaelic–English dictionary later, however, the name translated as something like 'large, grey, conical hill', which was rather more prosaic than I'd expected, and which certainly didn't do justice to the view that was widening and opening out during my ascent. It was now magnificent: mountain after mountain peak, some still snow-covered, as far as the eye could see to the east, and the turquoise sea and numerous islands to the west. I was hoping to see eagles too. My romantic notion was to stay on the mountain top for the night and hopefully wake with the eagles soaring around me in the dawn.

But within a few minutes of my reaching the top, the midges had found me. The weather was also looking like it might change; there was haziness in the sky to the west, which became a diaphanous veil of white. The cloud took form only very gradually, thickening into a grey shroud, so I couldn't be certain what the weather was going to do. It was midsummer and the days were long that far up north. Even though it was late afternoon, almost early evening, I would still have several hours sitting there with the midges until it would be time for sleep, and it was getting cold too. Should I stay up there and risk the weather, or was it better to make my way back down now? I had to decide whether to stay or go.

I decided to go. But there was a pang of regret. In coming down early was I missing the point, which was just to sit there, do nothing, allow what would happen to happen, and take whatever the elements threw at me? Was I just taking the easy option and avoiding discomfort? I also felt disappointment as I had not seen any eagles.

The return journey would be another twelve miles and I was already tired out, though I also knew it didn't get completely dark till about 11pm and I probably had time enough to get back. I needed to get off the ridge at the right point. If I didn't then I would end up on scree slopes and be in trouble, or, at the very best, have an extremely difficult and slow time getting down. I didn't want to be scrambling down scree in darkness. So I was descending very carefully, examining my map, and trying to read every contour and feature of the mountainside.

Just then an eagle flew over my head, looking down and calling. It was much closer than I had ever been to an eagle before.

It had white patches on its wings and tail, so it was probably a two-year-old, not yet fully mature. It was circling, picking up on the thermals, lifting effortlessly above me, and then it drifted from one side of the ridge to the other. It floated, smooth and easy, on what was, to me, an invisible medium. Its outspread body sensing the rippling air, the eagle coasted on a current I could neither see nor feel, till it dropped out of view.

I took this to be a sign that coming down off the mountain had been the right decision. Another voice in me asked why it was a sign that I'd made the right decision, and not a sign that it had been the wrong one, and that I should stay up longer and perhaps see more eagles. I decided that my first response had been the genuine intuition; the second was just a cynical backlash. It was interesting that I had this kind of thought process. I am not inclined to literally believe that things are 'signs' in this way. But the fact that those sorts of thoughts occurred to me showed, I think, how important being up on the mountain was to me, how much feeling was bound up with the decision to stay or go. And I do believe such intuitions are saying something that is 'true', even if they have nothing to do with the intentions of creatures around me in the wild. Seeing the eagle up on Sgurr na Ba Glaise completed the experience of the day for me; I had witnessed an eagle soaring close by and done what I had set out to do. There was a sense of conclusion and fulfilment.

My descent was tough – particularly tricky was finding the correct subsidiary off the main ridge that would bring me down into the right valley. I was tired and it was mentally as well as physically demanding. There was a huge effort and discipline involved in keeping my concentration step by step after so many miles of walking, in order not to lose my footing, or twist an ankle, and to avoid making rushed decisions and possibly losing my way. Even once back down in the valley I still faced a long walk back. By now it was raining, not hard, but a steady drizzle, and there was a haze of mosquitoes and midges. Long planks of larch had been placed on the ground to make a path across the bog. My hips were sore, as though I could feel them grinding in their sockets. My feet throbbed and my legs felt like lead drainpipes. Six miles still to go. All I cared about now was keeping going. I was just a weary body dragging one foot in front of the other.

In the dusky light I passed cattle and they gave me a long look, wondering what I was doing there. There were red deer also, and I got quite close to two of them. They stopped and stared, watching me with unwavering and total attention: heads rotated, eyes focused, ears alert and switched my way. Eventually they turned and ran with powerful movements up the steepness of the hill. In my own limbs, numbed as they were, I could still sense the strength and agility in their bodies.

I got back about 11pm. Undoubtedly I had made the right decision to come down. The rain had become heavier; by now I would not have been able to see anything up on that hilltop. The next morning the cloud had lowered even more; there would have been no magical views of eagles, and it would have been quite dangerous finding my way down. Exhaustion and ecstasy: I ached all over and, at the same time, I was fulfilled, content, and happy.

It was now over a year since my father had died, and I was having some solitary time at a place called the Hermitage, up in the west of Scotland. This was an old gamekeeper's lodge near the shores of a loch. I guessed it had been built in the early twentieth century; it was old enough to be fitted out with old-fashioned gas lamps, and there was no electricity except from a solar panel. The building was rendered with concrete-grey pebble-dash, had a verdigris-green metal roof, and pink roses grew up the walls. It felt tucked away: sited in the corner of a field, set back from the loch, with a backdrop of tall trees, at the end of a mile-long farm track. Beyond it there were no human habitations, roads, phone masts, fields, or planted forests for fifteen miles. There was just oak woodland, moorland, and the mountains dropping into the plunging depths of the loch. If I walked from the cottage over the meadow to the loch, I met it at the point where there was a little inlet or cove.

I was renting the Hermitage from a man named Giles, who lived in the south-east of England, but who came up here regularly. Some years ago he'd had a vision of creating a space where people could stay on retreat, a haven of quiet and peacefulness. He had written to sixty-three Highland landlords, asking if any of them had a suitable place that they would be happy to lease. He got twenty-two replies. Ten were friendly messages saying that, though they didn't have anything to suggest, they hoped he'd find somewhere satisfactory. The other twelve did make various offers. Most were impractical, suggesting, for example, that he might rebuild an old pile of stones, which used to be a sheep pen, sited halfway up a mountain. But a couple of them were more promising and, in the end, Giles had taken out a twenty-year lease on this one.

He had to do a lot of work renovating it, putting in a little wood-burning stove and solar panels, and creating a basic but comfortable dwelling, which became known as the Hermitage. It was a labour of love, and courageous of him to have seen through this vision, and also generous of him to have gladly shared it with others. Giles had been surprised by the high response rate he received to a blind mail-out of Highland landowners; he felt he got a genuinely sympathetic response and that his vision had struck a chord with many of them.

There was a book in which visitors were invited to write something, and I read some of the entries. Some were from people on retreat, and on their own, for the first time in their lives. Like me in that caravan on the Llŷn Peninsula twenty years before, they described how their initial apprehension turned into feelings of freedom and joy. It was moving to read these accounts and be reminded of my own, earlier, experience.

I had arrived here about a week earlier and had walked down to the water's edge expectantly, keen to see what would be there. As I approached, however, the geese went still and suspicious, and then lifted themselves up and away, honking rustily. Another bird startled off so fast I couldn't even see what it was. A heron's big, broad wings wheeled it away, round the corner of the shore, out of sight. The creatures saw me coming and dashed away from me, leaving me an outsider. I paddled in the water, gasping at the cold, my feet sinking into the sand that sparkled enticingly emerald and gold. I leant over to see closer, but the wind ruffled the surface, obscuring my view. I put my socks and shoes back on, wobbling on one leg and nearly losing balance as I put the sock back on the other. I felt clumsy and numb-headed, spaced out after my long drive north. I'd not really arrived, not yet tuned in. I was on the wrong frequency, crashing about in a hiss of white noise.

As is typically the case at the start of a retreat, for the first few days the habitual mind chuntered on as usual. It was like a child scrawling messages inside my head, scribbling the same message over and over again, and making an illegible mess of scribble.

It was time for what a friend of mine calls 'disciplined idleness'. Time to do nothing. Lots of nothing. Just to sit with a cup of tea and gaze out the window, and not to do anything, say anything, prove anything, be anything, find anything, solve anything, or any other type of anything. It was time to have a complete holiday from all that, to take a complete break from having to be 'me'. I could store the masks and uniforms, the badges and name tags, the job descriptions and to-do lists away at the bottom of a cupboard. I could forget that they were even there. I could allow myself to just sit there, simply watching the world go by, to rest and relax. This was the 'idleness' part of the practice.

'World is crazier and more of it than we think'

I didn't find it easy to do nothing, certainly not to begin with. In fact, doing nothing was surprisingly, even fiendishly, difficult. There was a tendency to distract myself: to make some toast, to pick a book off the bookshelf and flick through the pages, or, having only just arrived, to start planning my return journey. I would remember some detail I hadn't mentioned in an email, or else think of something that I ought to have done before I left home. I tried not to worry about such details, to forget them. I told myself: you are not as indispensable as you like to think and others can manage perfectly well without you. I resisted the temptation to distraction. This was the 'disciplined' part of the practice. Then came a phase of sinking through layers of different moods: boredom, anxiety, a tinge of despair, restlessness, lethargy, more boredom. But gradually something else came shining through.

It took time for the internal chatter to quieten, and only then could I really hear the birds singing, or the wind in the trees talking. But, several days later, my experience had changed and I was much more fully 'there' and astonished by how alive the place was. I watched black-throated divers on the loch with their young. Once or twice a white-tailed eagle swooped by in the distance. At dusk, red deer that usually roamed the hillsides came to graze on the more tender grass that grew lower down. A badger shuffled about outside the house in the half-light; it worked quickly, upturning stones or thrusting its paw into the ground, looking for worms and grubs. Along the shoreline of the loch an oystercatcher defended its nest against a raven. The high-pitched call – *kleep! kleep!* – of an oystercatcher is loud but rather squeaky, sounding uptight. Its bright orange eye also looks permanently startled and nervous. But, despite appearances, the oystercatcher was plucky, scolding shrilly at the raven, which was bigger than it, and dive-bombing it repeatedly. The raven eventually sloped away.

One day I went into the outhouse where the coal and wood fuel were stored and I disturbed a pine marten that was rummaging around. It scampered up onto the wooden beams above my head, protesting noisily, and we looked at each other. It clearly didn't know what to do. My guess was that it had come in through a gap under the door and now, standing in the doorway, I was blocking its escape. There was a wide open gap in the wall through which it could have made a getaway, but it didn't seem to notice this. So I moved further into the outhouse, towards the pile of firewood that I wanted, also thinking this would make space for the pine marten to get out of the door. But it panicked, squealed, and rushed up to the apex of the roof where there was a small gap. Desperately it squeezed itself into the space and just about managed to fit itself in. There it stayed: it evidently thought that if it couldn't see me then I couldn't see it. What the pine marten didn't realize was that its large, bushy tail was hanging down out of the hole in the roof, clearly visible. I could have even reached up and gently tweaked its tail. But I didn't do that; I collected my wood and retreated, leaving the door open so it could escape. When I peeked in an hour or so later, the pine marten had gone.

There were also bats in the roof of the house. I could hear them chattering at certain times of the day, sounding busy and excited like starlings, only more muffled. If I'd not been told there were bats up there I would have guessed it was swallows nesting in the gutters, chatting and chirruping. I didn't find the sound disruptive or unpleasant; the smell was less welcome, though even that wasn't too bad. I went to investigate where the bats came out at night; it was from a tiny crack in the rendering just above one of the windows. They are like mice in the way they can fit through a gap much smaller than you'd think possible. There was only room for them to come out one at a time. Each one would squeeze through the gap and plop out into the air, and only then the wings would open, and they'd fly.

They made immediately for the trees at the back of the house, suddenly in their element, hurrying, restless like children let out into a playground after too long in a classroom. They jerked and flickered like an old black-and-white film. They might seem erratic and spasmodic in flight, but they could be fast and direct when they wanted. I counted as each one appeared in the little hole, paused, and then plunged into mid-air. Out came a series of about half a dozen, then there was a pause, and after a while a few more emerged. I was expecting twenty or so, but more came, and still more. After half an hour I had counted up to 268. There were still a few faint murmurs from inside the roof, so I guessed it was a colony of about 300.

A bat can only see an inch in front of its face. But by echolocation it can fly all night, flitting around the branches of the trees, gobbling flies and midges, and then making its way back to exactly the right spot – that tiny gap in the wall and the safety of its roosting place.

The next day a swallow landed on the outside window ledge as I was sitting inside drinking a cup of tea. I leant forward so that my face was up to the glass and the swallow only a few inches away on the other side. It may have been a fledgling, and the other swallow that had now landed on the guttering above may have been its parent. It was tiny and delicate looking, just a couple of ounces of throbbing life. On top it was night-blue, nearly black. The feathers were fine, downy, almost like mole fur. Underneath it was off-white, looking rather scuffed and smudged. There was a chestnut-orange blur on its throat. The wings were huge relative to the rest of it, two dark crescents curving past the side of its body, pressing down into the concrete ledge. It quivered with quick, short breaths, and looked much smaller, more flimsy, on the window ledge than a swallow looks in the air.

It cocked its head; its jet-black bead of an eye examined a rusty nail that lay on the window ledge, then peered over the edge, then checked up at the gutter where its parent was watching. It flew as suddenly as it had landed. It just flicked off the ledge, switched between the house and the lime tree, swung to the height of the house, wings held taut in a great curve, rising up and then swivelling back again, the force of the swing pressing the wings outwards, till, with more fast flicks, it straightened, flowed up over the roof, and was gone.

In the northern hemisphere swallows, as well as swifts and martins, are part of our myth of spring and summer. 'They're back – which means the globe's still working', as Ted Hughes wrote in his poem 'Swifts'.[23] Although, according to the proverb, one swallow does not make a summer, I'm always surprised at just how joyful I feel when I see the first swallow of the year. Perhaps this is a response buried deep within us, and one that we have inherited from ancestors who lived at a time when the coming of summer really mattered. If you had lived for months in the gloom of long nights and freezing cold conditions, subsisting on salted meat and stale bread, then imagine the deep relief and joy you would feel at the first signs of summer. Even the merest touch of sun on the skin on an early spring day can bring an involuntary smile to my face.

Sometimes, in the last light around the Hermitage, the bats and swallows would hawk for flies around the same group of trees outside. A few times I saw them nearly crash into one another, though at the last instant they always avoided a collision. The bat would zigzag, lurch off to one side. It made me think of being in a car with an erratic, terribly speedy, taxi driver in rush-hour traffic. Was it just luck we got out alive, or did he, somehow, actually know what he was doing? The swallow simply swivelled its body, so that the wind immediately carried it off in the opposite direction. It was like a sailing boat tacking into the wind, only completely smooth and instantaneous.

Imagine us flying round fast with our eyes shut tight. Except that we can call out and hear our own echoes. If an echo comes back to us, there is an object coming up. If it comes back quickly, then the object is coming up fast. We are so good at this that we can build up a 'picture' of the world out of our echoes. We can swerve that swallow, skedaddle round the chimney pot, snap up miniscule flies. We call out, and a voice responds, telling us all we need to know about the world. A tree answers back louder and quicker as we approach; each branch, each twig, each leaf is a whole host of called-out questions and bounced-back replies. There is a sudden shout as another creature flies into our path, but it is our own voice that is warning us. Our world is made of echoes, made of our own voice's reflections, made of call-and-response in the night-time, made of sounding and rebounding. No wonder bats move so jerkily, so seemingly erratic.

J.A. Baker's *The Peregrine*[24] is widely recognized as a classic of nature writing. Baker, an unknown and obscure figure from a very ordinary background, devoted ten years of his life to observing the peregrine falcons that wintered around the woods and estuaries a few miles from his home in Essex. His book has an added urgency and poignancy because peregrines were, at that time in the 1950s and 1960s, an endangered species – persecuted by humans and poisoned with agricultural pesticides. *The Peregrine* contains astonishingly vivid and poetic writing, but it is based around observations of just one species of bird, within a modest-sized area of countryside that Baker explored on foot or by bicycle.

He describes moments of utter exhilaration watching peregrines:

> This mastery of the roaring wind, this majesty and noble power of flight, made me shout aloud and dance up and down with excitement.[25]

Baker was the manager of the local branch of the AA and later manager of a soft-drinks depot. In my mind's eye I see an ordinary middle-aged man, pedalling furiously on his pushbike round the country lanes of Essex, ecstatic in pursuit of the hawk. Part of the appeal of this image, and the humour of it, is that I can see myself in it too. Wild places and animals can kindle a sense of sheer wonder, an almost childlike delight and joy. Like the poet John Clare, we love 'wild things almost to foolishness'.[26]

The fastest, most powerful creatures and the most immense and wild landscapes can trigger awe. But even a tiny creature like a swallow can evoke amazement. I had hours to sit and watch the swallows round the Hermitage. In the sunlight, the feathers on their backs shone metallic blue. It was like watching a firework display; one suddenly appeared round the house and I gasped and craned my neck to see it, just catching a brief, splendid glimpse before it had gone. I marvelled that this tiny thing, weighing no more than sixty grams, had flown 6,000 miles from mid-Africa to reach here. A swallow might live for four or five years, and in that short life fly the equivalent of several times round the planet. It seemed almost incredible that such a fragile little creature could do such a thing. Even a swallow can astonish us, despite all our human sophistication, our seeming ability to do whatever, and go wherever, we please.

And how do they find their way; how do swallows migrate thousands of miles across land and sea, flying night and day, and coming back year after year to the same place? It has long been a mystery to humans how they do it, but scientists now believe that migrating birds use the sun and stars to navigate and also that they have in-built sensitivity to the earth's geomagnetic field. Their eyes contain special proteins that enable them to 'see' that magnetic field and then, somehow, they are able to 'read' it and find their way around the globe.

What is it like to be a migrating swallow? What would it feel like to follow the magnetic field of the earth? Would it be like having a compass built into our very being and, at a certain season, instinctively following where it is pointing? Our heart says 'north' and off we go. We are drawn on by a magnetic attraction, a subtle force that tugs at us, an inner calling that we cannot ignore. On and on we are pulled, for thousands of miles, over deserts and cities, mountains and seas. When we arrive we are soon busy nest building, breeding, raising young. But it won't be long before our heart will say 'south' and off we will fly again.

I noticed that male cuckoos were also calling from the trees around the Hermitage. By now, the females would have laid their eggs in another bird's nest. It wouldn't be too long before the adult cuckoos would depart for Africa; they leave much earlier than most other migrating birds. The young cuckoo in the nest would be raised by another species of bird – a dunnock or a meadow pipit perhaps – and then, all alone, never having had any contact with other cuckoos, it would find its way to central or southern Africa.

As I watched the swallows looping round my rooftop and pondered on them and the other creatures around this place, it opened me up to another layer of astonishment and wonder. Every living thing is a whole world of mystery. Like a tiny swallow sensing its way through the empty sky, other creatures use sense faculties that we do not have. They 'see' things we cannot see; they know things we cannot know. They have experiences of this world that are not available to us, that we can only try to imagine. To the degree we share the same sense faculties, our worlds overlap; but there are also regions of this world, spectrums of possible experience that, for us, are not directly knowable, that are shrouded in mystery.

There are seventy octaves of electromagnetic radiation, including seventeen octaves just within the infrared part of the spectrum. Humans are sensitive to less than one octave – what we call 'light', or at least 'visible light'. But many other parts of the spectrum are visible to other creatures. Watching the bumble bees visiting the Hermitage garden, I knew that they were able to see ultraviolet light; the white of a rose was a whole different experience to them from the white of the hawthorn blossom.

A barn owl hunted by night, largely using its faculty of hearing. The feathers on its round owl face are designed to direct as many air vibrations as possible into its ears. Out in the night, we humans would be able to locate approximately where a sound originated – whether it was down at our feet, or over to the left. With our two ears, one on each side of the head, our mind can compare the sound waves that reach each eardrum, and we can get a rough idea of where that noise came from – enough to turn and flash our torch in that direction and hope we'll be able to see what we're looking for. The barn owl has, like us, ears on the left and right of its head. But it also has one of these eardrums set slightly higher than the other, and one of them set slightly further forward in its head. This means that it will not only detect the tiniest sound, but also pinpoint its source with absolute accuracy. Not only will the owl hear the slightest rustle of leaves made by a mouse, but it will know *exactly* where the mouse is. The precision of the barn owl's hearing means it can find the mouse even in the dark. It doesn't just hear more sound than we do; it hears it in more dimensions. It lives in an entirely different soundscape, one not immediately knowable by us, a world of sound-locations.

A human nose has about 5 million olfactory receptor cells, whereas the red fox that lives on the wooded hillsides behind the house has something like 200 million. A fox lives in a world of smell. Things that, to us, have no smell at all, to a fox have distinct and individual aromas. This sensitivity to scent tells it not just about what is there, right now in the present, but also about what *was* there – that a rat crossed over this path yesterday and then went up that riverbank, that an otter marked out its territory by these trees, or that badgers played here earlier, and that some were male and some female. We humans may be able to infer, to work out rationally, some things about the past through what we see and hear around us in the present; creatures that live in an olfactory world smell it directly. To them, yesterday still stinks: the past is still present. They can sniff out clues, or pick up signs, undetectable by humans. Their world is redolent with messages from the past, a dimension of the world to which we tend to be completely oblivious. It is like a world in which little notes, reminders, messages have been jotted down and left lying around. Post-it notes are pinned to tree trunks, a name and an arrow pointing the way are scrawled across a pathway. But the animals need to read the messages quickly; once the rain falls the ink will blur and be much harder to decipher.

Salmon return to the loch near the Hermitage and then seek out exactly the same stream where they were born. Here they will breed and then die; it is a journey through sea and upriver for thousands of miles that they will make just once in their lifetime. How do they know which way to go? They can 'taste' their way to their native beck from halfway across the world. The ocean is, to them, full of subtle streams and watery seams, some of which have the flavour of home. These are dimensions of the ocean that remain completely hidden to creatures like us; places in which we are way out of our depth.

Peter Redgrove was a poet who also had a scientific background and training. In his book *The Black Goddess and the Sixth Sense*[27] he hypothesizes that, whilst there are many varieties of sensory perception, we humans have lost our sensitivity to most of them, our visual sense and then our sound sense having become overwhelmingly predominant. Our other faculties are like limbs that have withered through being forgotten about and underused. Animals, however, are still attuned to these 'invisibles' – all the many other frequencies, atmospheres, rhythms, radiances – and we can learn from them. We may, to some extent, still have these faculties, but they have gone unconscious or subliminal, and we may not know about them, or trust our own intuitions.[28] An example, one that is known about, and even studied scientifically, is the sensitivity some people have to the weather. We speak of being 'under the weather', that strange and seemingly inexplicable feeling of lethargy, muzzy-headedness, or moodiness when we get out of bed some mornings. Some people, however, are physically and emotionally affected by changes in air pressure, or changing light, or wind patterns. They really are, quite literally, under the weather.

I once suffered from ears that had become completely blocked up with wax, and this got so bad that I was virtually deaf for a couple of days. Luckily I was then able to attend a doctor's surgery and have my ears syringed. Walking home afterwards, everything sounded so fresh and keen. The sleeves of my coat swished against the sides of my body like cymbals crashing. But, if I held my arms still, I could also hear a tinkling noise like the peal of tiny bells: clear, crisp, and rather beautiful. At first I couldn't tell what was making such a delightful sound, but eventually I saw that it occurred at the same time as when the wind gently blew the leaves right at the top of the trees on the other side of the road. I knew there was no way I would normally have noticed such a thing, especially above the other sounds that were going on, such as passing cars, and people talking.

I realized that my ears detect those sorts of signals all the time, but that my mind sifts through and organizes the raw data that is given to it, picking out and prioritizing what it feels is important. Ordinarily, my mind simply filtered out the delicate rustling of the trees. Being unable to hear for a couple of days had, however, temporarily suspended the filtering mechanism. Now I could hear again, for about an hour, before 'normality' reasserted itself, my awareness of my surroundings was strangely altered.

Coming back down from a day up in the mountains I am often surprised by the zest and juiciness of the green of meadow grass and the leaves on the trees. Up above the tree line, my visual faculty becomes accustomed to a different colour-scape, a palette of browns and greys. It is almost a shock to suddenly encounter succulent greens again. But it is also welcome and familiar, as when one returns from foreign lands pleased to be home once more. I am grateful for green: its lushness, softness, coolness, and shade.

Walking on the hillside at dusk the rust-red of last year's bracken has become an orange glow. It shines so much that it stands out; it seems to rise up out of the ground and actually be hovering above the other plants and foliage. This is because in darker conditions my eyes have become more sensitive to red light. Human night vision can be much more rich and acute than we realize, but in our modern world of street lighting we can lose touch with this faculty. Robert Macfarlane has described this whole other world that we may miss out on:

> At night, new orders of connection assert themselves: sonic, olfactory, tactile. The sensorium is transformed. Associations swarm out of the darkness. You become even more aware of landscape as a medley of effects [...] The landforms remain, but they exist as presences: inferred, less substantial, more powerful.[29]

It is well known that blind people can develop extraordinary powers of hearing. My mother used to teach blind students. One day one of them hadn't turned up to the class, and my mother wondered aloud where she was. One of the other students replied that she was just on her way, and that she'd just crossed the road by the pelican crossing. Most of us would not even notice the sound of footsteps twenty yards down the street, let alone know who they belong to.

We can only know what is 'out there' through our senses and mind. Our knowledge and experience of it is therefore dependent on the particular sense faculties and mental processing that we employ. To that extent, what is 'out there' in and of itself, separate from us perceiving it, is always beyond us, inherently mysterious.

But nor are we totally separate and cut off from 'out there'; we have all the richness of our experience, which arises through connection and reciprocity. 'World' is a relationship, a negotiation. World is an arising of appearances; we humans divide this into an 'inner perceiving' aspect and an 'outwardly perceived' aspect, and we think of one as a thing that we call 'mind' and the other as a thing we call 'matter'. But we never experience either of these by itself, separately or independently; what we experience is always a relationship.

Humans, with our self-consciousness, separate the 'inner perceiving' and 'outwardly perceived', but in animals these are less separate, more part of one and the same experience. You can sense this when you watch animals watching you: they just stand still and stare, totally *in* that experience, so much so that they *are* that experience. There is much less of them removed from it, or reflecting on it as we can do.

Perception is not 'objective' in the sense of simply taking in what it is there and presenting it to us. As we've seen, is it conditioned by the particular sense faculties that we have, and the type of sensory information that is therefore available to our minds. But it also arises out of complex psychological processes, involving selection, interpretation, and making assumptions to fill in gaps in the sensory information. To do all this we use memories and what we have learnt culturally, as well as what comes to us more instinctually. Animals, as well as having different sense organs from us, will also have different inner processes of perception.

The result is that we all live, in a sense, in different worlds. Other creatures have experience that we have no access to, and we also have experience that is a mystery to them. Again, when I'm most alert to the land, and to the creatures dwelling in it, I'm returned to the awareness that every living thing is a whole world of mystery. So often, however, I tend to assume that the world really is how it appears to me. I look at the view outside my window and I think that is how it actually is. But what I see is only one angle on the world, one particular take, one of many possible perspectives. The view out my window is not really like that at all, or at least it is not *just* like that. 'World is crazier and more of it than we think', as a line from a poem by Louis MacNeice has it.[30] And it is not only that there is more to the world than we know; there is more to the world than we *can* know. Of course we know rationally that there are unseen aspects to the world; science can tell us about the earth's magnetic field, or infrared electromagnetic radiation, and this knowledge can be a wonderful thing. It is thanks to science that we can have some inkling of, for example, how birds migrate. But it is not the same as experiencing and sensing directly, the way a particular animal may be able to. There is more to the world than we think.

In a book for budding writers Ted Hughes advises that if you want to capture the essence of a thing in words you need, above all, to imagine it vividly:

Just look at it, touch it, smell it, listen to it, turn yourself into it. When you do this, the words look after themselves like magic. [...] You will read back through what you have written and you will get a shock. You will have captured a spirit, a creature.[31]

If we want to try to imagine the life of another creature, we need to 'just look at it' as Hughes suggests. But in order to 'turn yourself into it', to become that creature, you need to not only look *at* it, but also try to imagine how *it* looks – and how it hears, smells, touches, and tastes. How does that animal perceive the world; what kind of world does it live in?

Of course we can only *try* to imagine this. What we imagine won't really be like what it is like. We won't know what it's like, for example, for a bat to be a bat, but more like a human being

123

pretending to be one. But that attempt to imagine can still take us out of ourselves, out of our human-centric view of the world, and closer to the mystery of another creature.

The peregrine falcon is, of course, a hunter; it lives by swooping down and killing other birds. A peregrine's eyes are much larger relative to ours, and when they focus on an object their vision can have a resolution eight times more powerful. As J.A. Baker explains in his study of the peregrine:

> a hawk, endlessly scanning the landscape with small abrupt turns of his head, will pick up any point of movement; by focusing on it he can immediately make it flare up into larger, clearer view.

Then, so beautifully, he goes on to imagine how a creature with such vision would experience the world:

> the peregrine lives in a pouring-away world of no attachment, a world of wakes and tilting, of sinking planes of land and water. We who are anchored and earthbound cannot envisage this freedom of the eye. The peregrine sees and remembers patterns we do not know exist [...] He may live in a world of endless pulsations, of objects forever contracting or dilating in size [...] Everything he is has been evolved to link the targeting eye to the striking talon.[32]

Baker does not anthropomorphize the peregrine, nor is he anthropocentric. As far as it is possible, he is able to imagine the world of this other creature, able to envision its vision, its view of the world. This empathy, this sympathetic awareness, is one reason why Baker's *The Peregrine* is such a classic of nature writing.

I loved my time at the Hermitage. By the time I came to leave the grass had grown up around the wheels of my car. On my daily walks along the edge of the loch I had reconnected with the sense of stillness and contentment that I had felt at Trwyn a few years back and at Waingap some years earlier. This place was also vibrantly alive. I could more vividly appreciate the numerous wild creatures living their lives around me. I was literally surrounded: a pine marten in the outhouse, a badger's sett just yards from the front door, wrens nesting under the gutter, hundreds of bats in the roof, and swallows circling the house all day long, like electrons whizzing round the nucleus of an atom. I wondered if, once, everywhere in Britain thronged with life in this way. For me, as on previous solitary retreats, it had felt important to tune in to that aliveness, to realize that our human world isn't the only world, to try and really, deeply imagine the unknown, unknowable world of swallows, bats, salmon, foxes, and the many other creatures.

One thing that happens in the process of meditating is that we see how our experience is 'mind-made'; it is very strongly conditioned and created by our own desires, attitudes, interpretations, or expectations. Now I was looking outwards and imagining in a different way the mind-made nature of world: how, since there were many kinds of mind, there were many kinds of world, and our human one wasn't the only one, or the one that was most true, or real, or objective.

Back at Waingap I had touched into an awareness that was more 'participative', more empathic of the life and creatures around me. At the Hermitage I found myself reflecting on this yet more deeply, trying to imagine, and relate to, the sensing and perceiving, and the resultant experience, of those creatures. We talk about 'really being there', but what is 'there' is a mystery. 'World is crazier and more of it than we think.'

9

Green fire

Mean March day in Cornwall; bitter cold, sullen. The mud of the riverbed, exposed by the outgoing tide, was smooth and dull like a sheet of aluminium, though the water glittered like chrome. The sky was a lead lid slammed shut, deadpan and heavy. It had been raining for days, but this morning the rain had let up and I decided to get out and go for a walk. The woods were quiet, subdued, tensed against the bone-biting cold, trying to conserve energy. A pheasant, invisible in the undergrowth, coughed dryly three times. A blackbird muttered repeatedly, *chink-chink-chink*, like a child tapping a glass bottle with a spoon. I disturbed some woodpigeons and they flew off with a clatter of wings, startlingly loud in the silence. Then the woods went quiet again; a stony cold silence in the stony cold stillness.

The old bracken had collapsed exhausted by the side of the path. Brambles trailed like a tangle of discarded electric cables; the current in them had been cut off long ago. The trees seemed stiff, inert, lifeless. It was difficult to believe in the possibility of spring, though there were primroses quiet at the feet of the trees.

I slipped and slid along muddy tracks, up and out of the woods and then down towards the coast path. The cloud had thinned a little; sunlight flared through in patches, a soulless and colourless light, bleached blue-white, like the flare of burning magnesium.

Sometimes more light managed to slant through. I was starting to appreciate the effect of that muted silver light on the tones of the landscape. Then, suddenly, just for a moment, the sun was full out. Everything turned hard and shiny, glaring and glittering.

Down by the sea the mood was wild and stormy. I watched a kestrel contend with the wind. It tried to hover above the cliff top but was thrust back through the air for twenty yards, still in the same open-winged posture, as though an invisible hand reached out and pushed it roughly backwards. The kestrel managed to turn itself, as if to fly away, but then, with the wind behind it, it was hurtled downwards towards the brown ruts of a ploughed field. I thought of Ted Hughes watching his hawk in the rain, thinking of the day it would

meet the weather
Coming the wrong way,
and get smashed to the ground, its heart blood mixed
    'with the mire of the land'.[33]

But, for now, this hawk turned again into the wind and recovered itself. It managed to hold its position, hung in suspense above the field, wings splayed right out, tail fully fanned. Looking from one side, I could see that the tail was actually curved back in at the bottom, held taut, wind taut. The kestrel clasped the sky, grasped the air, gripped the wind, holding on for dear life. The bird's wings held tight, they merely quivered rather than flapped, making only the slight but vital adjustments needed to keep its position steady. All the time it looked keenly downwards. The eyes of kestrels can detect trace marks left on the ground by the urine of voles and small mammals; this is one of their ways of closing in on their prey.

Below the headland, where the trees grew sideways, the sea was running and jumping, screaming and cursing at the black rock. Turning a corner and moving into the full force of the wind was like walking smack into a block of ice. I thought I heard human voices in the sea's howling. When I got back home the skin on my face felt scoured, but also rosy and healthy. Inside my head, though, I could still hear those whining, windy voices.

During the last three days there had been non-stop storm and rain and I had been holed up, only dashing outside to collect another stash of firewood from the shed. The rain thrashed across the sky, driving, drilling rain that would have had me drenched in minutes. I ended up watching the drops dribble down the big window panes. As they drizzled, their surface tension attracted them towards each other; they zigzagged across the glass, merging, forming bigger, heavier drops that then slid faster towards the bottom of the pane.

There were three pigeons hunched up on the branch of a tree just outside, patiently sitting out the storm. They looked water-sodden, their plump pigeon shapes even more puffed up and swollen with rain. Only the gulls dared brave the wind and rain during these stormy days. The wind got right under them, lifted them vertically upwards, reversing the law of gravity. Often, and in calmer weathers, I had watched them, milk-white against the dark of the trees, drifting down the river valley, leisurely seeming, even languid, simply outstretching their wings and flowing along. There was just the occasional nudge of the wings, a slight fine-tuning of poise and posture, but otherwise they floated, smooth and liquid. Sometimes there was a great swirl of gulls, a slow whirlpool of a hundred or more of them, circling round and round each other, creating an unhurried rhythm and dance. They were completely silent whilst they circled and I wondered what this behaviour was about. Was it just for companionship, safety in numbers, or were they gathering together before flying off somewhere? The steadiness and quietness of their motion was like a prayer or ritual: slow, even solemn, repetitive, trance-like.

In the gale, however, it was different. They still relished flying, but the banking and balancing in the force of the wind needed more effort, both physical and mental.

On another afternoon during these stormy days, the rain softened, then stopped for a while, and I took the chance to walk outside. Loudly clacking jackdaws pinned back their wings and launched, torpedo-like, into the air. Crows paddled manically when there was a lull, otherwise just rode as best they could the force of the storm. A magpie, perched on a branch, cursed into the cold wet wind, and then flew with furious wing flaps in the opposite direction, its long tail cumbersome and ungainly. In the gale a heron struggled to fly from one side of the river to the other; it stumbled and hesitated, tottered like a drunken man trying to cross a busy road.

When I entered the woods the rain started up again. Soon my vision was blurred by raindrops on the lenses of my glasses, and my hearing muffled by the hood of my coat and the sound of raindrops falling on its fabric. I'd been cooped up indoors on my own for days, and finally I had managed to get out, only to have my sphere of awareness reduced to just a small radius around me. But, instead of regretting that, I managed to enjoy it. I savoured the cold, damp air in my nostrils, the dank, earthy smell of leaf litter, the coconut fragrance of the gorse blossom, and another sweet hyacinth-like smell whose source I couldn't locate.

I noticed how many things around me were rain-drenched. The beige trunk of a young ash tree was now like varnished chestnut, the silver-grey of beech had become black slate, and the grey-green of oak had turned dark chocolate. The oak was blotched with lichen, bluish-grey like the rind of stilton cheese. Dead bracken was bashed and bruised, flattened down by the pounding of rain. A clump of daffodils was a surprise of yellow against the drenched dark colours. The atmosphere in the woods was still now, except that drops of water splashed from the trees into the understorey, causing random leaves or twigs to suddenly twitch or shudder. The woods trembled in the aftermath of the storm.

Afterwards I sloshed back along the old holloway, the old lane that, in all this rain, had become a stream, spewing the detritus of the field and hedgerow: leaves, twigs, snags of branches, bits of bark, chips of stone, and the sole of an old shoe.

I was staying in a rather beautiful studio flat on the edge of a village in south Cornwall. Originally built as a large garage apart from the main house, it was used for a while as a stable for some children's ponies, after that rebuilt as a musician's workshop, and then converted again into a lovely studio flat. Some of the fixtures and fittings were taken from an old, decommissioned Norwegian fishing boat that the owners had bought a few years back whilst on holiday and then sailed back to England. The mast of the boat had become the central pillar of a spiral staircase in the flat; one of the portholes had become a window in the little bathroom. All along one side of the main room were big windows with a wide open view over the River Fowey and the woodlands and fields beyond. It was only a few miles to the sea and so the river was tidal, always changing. Every day I saw a river flowing to my left, then a big, full lake, then a river running rightwards, then an open, empty mudflat, and then a river running leftwards again.

I was on a sabbatical and had a three-month stay there, mostly by myself, and I was feeling very lucky and fortunate. The owners of the studio had kindly let me stay for a very reasonable rent. So I was seeing in the spring. The first few weeks, however, had been cold and wintry. A north-easterly had been blowing across the whole country for an unusually long time, bringing late snow and ice to many places. This strange wind seemed to freeze time, to hold spring at bay, to block the arrival of milder weather. After that initial wet period, there were a couple of weeks with virtually no rain, and that northeast wind was very drying.

One day I went for a walk on the nearby downs to see that several acres had burnt to the ground. The hillside was covered in a carpet of thick black charcoal. Firemen with rubber beaters were still stamping out the last traces of fire. In the following weeks there was to be speculation around the village about how the fire had started. One theory was that a certain person, taking matters into their own hands, deliberately started the fire to clear the ground so there would be more primroses the following year. But there was no way to prove this. For frogs and toads, lizards and snakes, insects and butterflies, and even birds and mammals it must have been deadly and destructive. Human waste that had been dumped in the undergrowth was now revealed amongst the cinders: bits of old ironwork, plastic trays charred and curled in the fire, even the chassis of an old car.

But the blackness was only a few inches thick. Sticking the heel of my boot in and pulling it back, rust-red leaf litter was revealed beneath. Within a couple of weeks, bluebells, albeit with stunted leaf tops, were shooting up again. Then grasses, rosebay willowherb, and a few thistles sprouted out of the charred crust. A week later stalks of bracken were poking through the charcoal and I saw a flock of twenty or so chiffchaffs feeding on the burnt ground.

Perhaps rather perversely, as spring finally edged its way in, I then noticed how much I loved the late winter. As the leaf buds plumped up, the trees on the far riverbank had a haze of subtle wintry colours: burgundy, creamy-beige, copper, and silver-brown. Sometimes the trees waved in the wind and I was reminded of gazing into rock pools where seaweeds swayed, intricate and delicate, embroidered from threads of coral-red and amber-brown.

The distant trees held, in a certain light, a faint glow. It was like a diaphanous pale skin forming over the bare bones of a skeleton structure. As the days of April progressed, the glow became more speckled, as though the trees had been dusted with light green powder. The trees shimmered – a gauzy shimmer, a pale intimation of what was to come. Then, although the ash trees were still grey and skeletal, the beeches began to be flecked with milky-green, and the oaks glowed with honey-green, golden and woody. As the leaves opened further, the trees began to reflect the sunlight; it glanced off the glossy new leaves and they shone with bright splashes of colour.

I wanted to press the 'pause' button, hold onto those beautiful colours, to savour them for a while longer. At the same time I was eager to 'fast forward' further into spring. My human mind craved both at once. I wanted to stop and hold on and, at the same time, I wanted to rush onwards and hoover up more of the experience.

A bend in the path, a clearing in the woodlands, or the crest of a hill triggered desire for more: maybe there would be a new corner of the woods to discover, or a bigger vista might open up, or an even more beautiful tree capturing even more of that golden sunlight. But, regardless of what I wanted, spring just danced on, skipping to its own rhythm, singing its own song.

The trees on that opposite riverbank were almost all late to leaf: some beech, but mostly ash and oak. The woods on my side of the river faced south and so the spring came quicker. Elder trees had been in leaf since March. Now, in April, looking up from beneath the trees, the shamble of soft browns and greys was scored with little notches of the most intense green. It was as though someone had cut little nicks through the fabric of the winter world, and green light was shining through. There was a fire of green: green flames that would soon burn and burst right through. Then the whole wood would ignite and be ablaze with green.

The blackthorn flowers began as pinpricks of white, snow-coloured embroidery that magically sewed itself, turning the trees into resplendent pearly kings and queens, the foamy white flowers gleaming against the dark black-purple juts and edges of the spiky branches. Hawthorn leaves were like green stars, tight little whorls of ultra-green. A little later, the greens of hazels and beeches were pure and translucent. The holly bush next to them appeared almost dark blue by comparison. Beech leaves especially caught and played with light; it filtered right through them, in contrast to the glossiness of sycamore or hawthorn. On a sunny day looking up into a beech tree was like gazing through a stained-glass window of intense green. On a duller day, the leaves seemed more calm, velvet, and silvery.

Soft yellow primroses had been out since March, and in late April were at their peak. The white star clusters of wild garlic had also opened; there was acid-yellow wood spurge, and the first few bluebells, with many more to come. Early red campion flowers were the most vivid purple-pink, as if dipped in a tin of printer's ink – pure magenta, vibrant against the creamy-lime of alexanders. The elegant shapes of ferns unfurled from the woodland floor; their green forms filigreed with gold, copper, and bronze threads that looked rough and fibrous, but that were actually soft and downy to touch. Bracken, bent double, untwisted and unclasped itself, like green fists unclenching.

And of course there was the birdsong. Blackcaps had arrived and their little bodies pulsated with hurried streams of song. The blackbird, by contrast, was more *largo* to the blackcap's *allegro*. It was often the bird that sang last at night, a song with repeated phrases, pauses, and variations. Goldfinches glissaded, quick, cascading lark-like song. I took to leaving the sliding door in my bedroom wide open, so that I would be woken by the dawn chorus the following morning.

As the trees filled out and took shape, the ground became strewn with catkins, wind-blown blossom petals, and various bits of wrapping and packaging that the leaves had arrived in:

copper coloured husks beneath the beech trees, coral pink from the sycamore, or thick black buds from the ash. Everything was uncurling, opening, then bursting forth and expanding outwards and upwards. And it all seemed to come from nothing. Within a matter of weeks, out of the darkness of winter, a vast canopy of new leaves had appeared over the woodlands, and fresh growth was shooting out of the ground and clambering exuberantly over the hedgerows. Where did it all come from? How did all that new material just manifest, seemingly from nowhere?

On a rational level I knew that, through the process we call photosynthesis, the plants were creating new living tissue out of carbon dioxide from the atmosphere and the power of sunlight, with the help of rainwater and a few minerals out of the soil. But it was still hard to fathom, difficult to believe that this huge multitude of leaves in the woods, the expanding and filling out of hedges along the lanes, all the bustling and burgeoning plant life in the fields were made just from carbon dioxide from the atmosphere and photons of light that had travelled 94 million miles from the sun. An invisible and intangible, odourless and colourless gas was becoming strong and solid, fibrous and textured, fragrant and multicoloured. Leaves and woody stems, branches, trunks, roots, flowers, and fruits were being conjured out of thin air. I had my reasons and explanations as to how all this change happened, but the changing-ness of things still took my breath away. I could not help being amazed at how those bright green flames of spring tore out of the cold darkness of winter.

Day after day I wandered about the woodlands enthralled. If I hadn't walked a particular way for a while, I'd retrace that path eagerly, wondering what new transformation would have taken place. It seemed there was some new miracle each day. I felt that if I closed my eyes for even a moment, or looked the other way at the wrong time, then I might miss some more magic. Each day was like a whole new life.

I was totally captivated by this place, absorbed in the coming spring. Maybe I had never in my life been so fully and consistently 'present' in a place as here in these glorious woodlands. I forgot all about my other life; it seemed like another world, far away and long ago. Except that two or three times, whilst out walking, strong feelings would rise to the surface of awareness, and I knew there was an inner transformation taking place; new ideas and perspectives were emerging, equally mysteriously, also materializing seemingly from nowhere. By the end of my time here in Cornwall I knew I was going to go home and quit my job. I had been in the post for about eight years and my experience of the job and the team I worked with had been good. It was, however, a style of working that I had known, semi-consciously, was running dry. Yet I had not found the courage or conviction to do anything about it – I just kept pushing down the doubts and resistance. But now, although I had not rationally and consciously made a decision, I became aware that, deep down, something had irrevocably changed. In the dark, deep soil of my being some new shoot was struggling, growing, and longing for sunlight. I could no longer ignore it, and pretend it wasn't there. Somehow, the decision had made itself.

An English wood in spring must be one of the most beautiful sights in the world. Sometimes my heart couldn't cope with all that beauty. The beauty was too big and my heart too small. It was like a huge current of energy conducted through a cable so frail it might fuse and burn out. Or it was like the full flood of a river poured into a tight little tube that might split and burst apart. There was so much beauty squeezing through such a tiny, narrow aperture. I unconsciously held on, instinctually and automatically attached to the experience, causing a constriction of the heart. It was a subtle, but fundamental, inner stance towards life, an ever-present tendency that I was becoming more conscious of. It was a grasping of the ungraspable. If only I could not clasp so tightly, not stifle the beauty, not futilely try to grab the flame. If only I could even more fully surrender to the spring, open my heart in abandon, allow the full glory of that green fire to come raging in, let myself be, 'swept away in the current of pure affirmation'.[34]

I loved that place by the river, and the nearby woodlands, and the rugged shore. There were many spots along the way that had become like dear friends. This gift of spring was so generous, so abundant that my heart flowed full of gratitude, it brimmed with wonder, even a sense of reverence. It wasn't some kind of 'Creator' that I was revering. The feeling of reverence was more a deep sense of wonder at the miracle of becoming, the mystery of birth and death, creation and destruction – that endless mystery that lies at the heart of everything. I had a strange and baffling sense of looking beyond the limits of reason to that which could only be wondered upon. Like those budding trees across the valley, life was a constant shimmering, arising and ceasing, growing and decaying. Life was a never-ending flickering in and out of existence, a strange and ungraspable river of coming and going, never stagnant, always pregnant, full of new possibility and potential. Life can be so utterly vivid and immediate, and yet it can never be pinned down or captured. It is a green fire that never stops burning, consuming all that goes before it, but then brilliantly glowing with new light.

10

The return journey

I am back in north-west Wales. Realizing how close I am to the place on the Llŷn Peninsula where I had my first taste of solitude just over twenty-five years ago, I have driven there to revisit the place and remember what it was like.

The caravan in the corner of the field is long gone. The farmland upon which it was sited is divided up into a number of small strips of meadowland, none of which contains a caravan, or any sign of one having once been there. I have to admit to myself that, rather to my surprise, I can't remember for sure which of those fields it was in.

I wander down to the coast and watch modest little waves licking the pebbles on the shore. Five oystercatchers swerve away from me, and a couple of ringed plovers hop on their spidery-thin legs from pebble to pebble, keeping me at a safe distance.

I walk back inland and gradually climb the mountain. The sun is straining through muslin cloud, but, even so, enough light sieves through to catch the colours of things. The rock is steel-blue, but peppered with spicy tones – nutmeg, cinnamon, cardamom – and blotched with lichen of turmeric yellow. The summit is like a wrecker's yard; rock stacked up into top-heavy heaps, rock tilting at precarious-looking angles, rock crushed and smashed, rock pulverized and spilling down the hillside. I cannot find the graffiti-daubed rock that had caught me by surprise twenty-five years ago. Probably a quarter of a century of rain and wind has etched away the paint.

It is the opposite end of the year to last time I was here. This present visit is taking place in late winter-early spring, rather than late summer-early autumn. The fields are full of sheep with newborn lambs and the gorse bushes, the most plentiful thing to grow around here, are volcanoes of blossom. From dirty-green sprawls of spikes have erupted flowers of pure, saturated yellow. The air is full of their sweet fragrance. The glory of the flowers doesn't seem to match the mean and scraggy look of the plant; it is as if butterflies were sprouting out of the barbed-wire fences.

The land feels somewhat familiar, and yet also strange and distant. Through the passing years my memory has patched together various images of this place, attempted to stitch a few scraps into a seamless whole. Now, walking round the landscape again, I see how fragmented those memories were. It is not that the memory falls completely apart at the seams; some things I do recognize and feel acquainted with, some things are more vaguely familiar, but other things are quite different from how I had remembered them, not at all what I had envisaged.

Since that fortnight I spent in the caravan in my early twenties I have taken time almost every year to be alone somewhere in nature. I cannot now imagine being without these times of solitude; they are an essential ingredient of my life. They are times for enriching, thickening, and deepening. They are a container for brewing and fermenting the mix of sweet malt and bitter hops that forms a life. Solitude is like time for the dough to rise; the longer you leave it, the tastier the bread. You can make a fast, one-rise loaf, and it will work, but the flavours won't be so good, not nearly so earthy, nutty, and wholesome.

Much of the time I live in a 'secondary reality'; I have a commentary going on inside my head, running through each and

140

every day. I tell myself a story about why that person makes my life so difficult, or how I would be really happy if only X, or Y, or Z. I explain and embellish what is happening to me. I often exaggerate those events I either strongly like or dislike. There is, of course, a place for reflection, interpretation, and stories. But what I mean by 'secondary reality' is automatic, habitual rumination that is unaware, undiscriminating, and unhelpful. Some of the stories are plain fantasy and they can become obsessive and self-fulfilling.

In their positive form, stories are one way we grow, how we develop a sense of ourselves, how we learn and become self-aware. But this other kind of story, that I am talking about now, is told not in order to learn, but in order to stubbornly entrench myself, to maintain and defend a sense of ego. The stories are like a tough skin, or armour that protects me from those things I find painful. I keep talking to myself as a kind of reassurance: I think therefore I am. In the thick of life these fabricated versions of reality can become very sophisticated and clever, subtle, but spun so tight I can hardly see they are there. And then I *become* the story; it gets right under my skin. I can no longer distinguish my interpretation from actual events; I am living in a secondary reality.

Get away from it all, however, and the web starts to unravel. I still hear the stories going on in my head, but the threads don't quite knot together anymore, they blow loose and start to look faintly ridiculous. I notice that the tone of the voice is whiny, or a touch prim, or rather overexcited. Times of solitude help me come back to the primary reality – to actual, felt experience, and then, eventually, to a more reasoned and balanced perspective on that experience. Likewise, nature helps bring me back to what is primary, to the senses and the body, back into what may be rawer, but also more real. Each time I dive deeper into the wilderness I can feel that green fire burning through me. I feel more alive: in the grind of my bones, in the thud of the blood, in the twitch of my nerves. Within me and without, I can sense the intense aliveness of life, the sheer urge of life to live.

But then I have to go back to my other life. There is the real challenge. How to stay alive in the hustle and hassle of the city? There are just more demands and distractions in the city, more stimuli to trigger my craving and aversion. How to return home and not slip straight back into that tough old skin? It will seem comfortable because it is reassuringly familiar. But it is worn and frayed, and rubs at the edges because it no longer fits. Far better to try and stay as I am in this new skin; it is tender, yes, but also healthy and glowing. Solitary practice isn't sufficient in itself; it is the going home that is the real test, the real practice. But, for me, times of solitude are vital, times to slough off the old skin and try out a new, fresher one.

We are cultured creatures, or creatures of culture. Humans have become urban, settled, civilized, sophisticated, and highly self-aware. But for most of the history of *Homo sapiens* we were nomadic hunter-gatherers, living in the wild. For vast spans of time, stretches of time that dwarf the period since the first settled agricultural civilizations, our experience and conditioning have been of living much more as part of nature. Humans have changed the way they live far more quickly than biological evolution has been able to keep pace with. Perhaps our nerves aren't yet evolved for cities; our senses aren't adapted to wholly human-built environments. And so we return to nature; from time to time we need to 'rewild' ourselves.

About 2,500 years ago, a young man called Gautama grew up in one of the fast-growing, bustling city states of north-east India. But, although he grew up in luxury, he found life in the city cramped and dusty and, in order to seek answers to his existential questions, he escaped from the city and went deep into the forest. Eventually he found the enlightenment he had been searching for, and became known as the Buddha. However, he did not stay in the forest; he went back to teach and help others. For the rest of his life he travelled between the villages, towns, and cities, a life on the road, a life of engagement with the society of his time. Eventually monasteries were founded on the edges of those urban areas, and there began to emerge a Buddhist culture that would eventually inspire a whole civilization.

But the Buddha also went back frequently to the forest. Even though he was already fully enlightened, there are many stories of him slipping away to meditate and to spend time alone in the green depths of the jungle. The earliest canonical texts record his encounters with wild animals, such as with a bull elephant that brought the Buddha water to drink in his trunk.[35] Whenever I read these texts I sense that the Buddha loved those wilderness places and felt an affinity with the creatures there, despite the potential discomfort or even danger.[36]

The Buddha lived both 'culture' and 'nature', he moved between the city and the forest, he combined and integrated two ways of living. On my own lower level, I feel my times of solitude are also about creating a relationship and a balance between culture and nature.

The Zen master Dogen was once asked what it would be like to be enlightened. He is reputed to have replied, 'It is to be intimate with all things.' In nature I have at least momentary glimmers of something akin to that. I am captivated by the world around me; I lose myself in my surroundings. I can become so absorbed that I forget the old world; the ambitions and ego projects, and the roles and self-identities bound up with them, fade and fall, like autumn leaves shaken from a tree. The defensive barrier of 'self' lowers, and then, there, is the world. The door swings open and a whole glorious world is waiting. Losing myself in that world, I find love and connection, gratitude, wonder, and reverence.

I wrote much of this book during my stay in that flat overlooking the River Fowey, just a few miles up from its mouth on the south Cornish coast. When I first arrived there I could hear a blackbird singing in the garden. Initially, however, it was as if I was 'outside' listening in, as though I was listening through a window with my ear pressed against the pane, and the song was slightly muffled and distant. But the more I listened, really listened, the closer in I got. I started to recognize the blackbird's singing as individual and distinctive. He used certain motifs (*hurdy-gurdy, hurdy-gurdy-woody*) that were quite different from those sung by the other blackbirds in the garden, and that he repeated in different combinations and with endless embellishments and variations. His song, with its trills and churrs, the pauses as if for thought, and then more melodious phrases, became very loved and familiar to me. And then I was no longer 'outside', no longer merely listening in.

I have a book featuring a reproduction of a painting of the Buddha by a contemporary Western artist.[37] The Buddha is walking through a forest, but has come to a stop. He leans down and gently reaches out towards a small bird on the ground just in front of him. The canvas is painted full of the browns and greens of the forest. But the Buddha is not painted: there is just an empty Buddha-shaped space, with the white of the canvas shining through. The Buddha is there, but also not there.

In the Buddhist tradition there is a well-known story about the Buddha encountering a dangerous elephant. The elephant had been kept in captivity and badly treated, so it was aggressive and angry. Then it had been released back into the wild near where the Buddha was walking in the forest. It charged at the Buddha, who heard it coming, but stood his ground and directed loving-kindness towards the rampaging wild animal. The elephant thundered through the undergrowth towards the Buddha, birds fled from trees and bushes, and the ground shook. Still the

Buddha stood, gazing unflinchingly at the elephant with eyes of loving-kindness. Just yards from the Buddha the elephant came to a stop. Those two great beings stood face-to-face, at peace with one another.[38]

This story is a parable of the power of loving-kindness. The Buddha's love was so strong that the elephant sensed the Buddha meant him no harm. Love overcame aggression and conquered the underlying fear and paranoia that fuelled that aggression.

A friend of mine has another interpretation of the story, though it is quite in keeping with the first explanation, perhaps just another way of saying the same thing. She says the elephant couldn't come crashing into the Buddha because the Buddha *wasn't there*. There was no hatred or fear in the Buddha, no noisy, protesting, frightened ego and therefore nothing, no one, to charge at. My friend says that when she is in nature she is also trying to disappear, to be not there. If she can be quiet and still and loving, then she can vanish and the world will appear as never before. She is trying to be like an empty space: an *empty* space as opposed to a *blank* space, a window through which the world can shine more than ever.

For the last week of my stay in that studio flat on the Cornish river there was fine weather, and the warmed-up air whispered of summer. I wanted to make the most of my remaining time, to spend the few precious days I had left getting in as close as possible to that beautiful place and the creatures that lived there. If I walked down to the harbour town and caught the little ferry boat across to the smaller town on the other side, I could then make my way east along the coast path. Along that seven-mile stretch of coast, before the next harbour town, there were no roads, no caravans, no farm buildings, not even pylons or phone masts.

Apart from one, tiny stone cottage perched atop a cliff, there was just farmland rolling down to England's edge, a borderland where the cultivated fields met with the rough cliff and the wild Atlantic Ocean. The shoreline was mostly rocky and inaccessible, but with the occasional sandy cove.

During that last week I decided to stay out for the night along this unspoilt and remote stretch of coast. Maybe something 'special' would happen; perhaps I'd see something amazing, have a close encounter with a bird or creature, and that would be a way of 'completing' my stay there. As the day grew dusky I found a spot to stay for the night. I sat and watched the waves and rocks as the detail dissolved into darkness; it blurred and smudged, became more flat and monochrome.

Oystercatchers called occasionally in their anxious, piping voices. Cormorants were fishing, flipping up from sitting position and going into the water almost vertically. A few gulls perched on rocks. They sat still and quiet, ready for the night. One stood up, stretched its wings, rotated on the spot, and sat down once more. There was something cat-like about the way it stretched and settled again, compact and contained, and the way it sat with its eyes open, but seeming aloof from its surroundings.

Whilst at first things seemed to just disappear into the blackness, as time went on my sensory awareness changed. In the absence of light, sounds became louder and clearer. The waves and buffets of wind seemed more sudden and closer up in the darkness. I felt warm and comfortable wrapped in my sleeping bag, though I didn't yet feel sleepy, so I continued watching and listening. Stars tried to shine through the patchy cloud. The thrift glowed in the dark like bristles of light. White sea campion and large, white daisy-like flowers also stood out, zooming out of the inky blackness. Earlier, in daylight, I'd noticed a nearby rock with blotches of blue-grey lichen. But now, in the almost dark, it looked like a rock with giant white spots. The sea was a metallic silver-blue, fairly calm, twitching and fidgeting, the odd wave crashing. There was another section of rock, a diagonal slant that in daylight had been slate-blue, but which in the dark seemed to leap forward, pale blue-green like a glacier, or a sheet of frosted glass, and faintly gleaming.

This experience was a bit like being part of a black-and-white photograph. In fact, it was like being in the negative, mostly black and dark, but with features that were white and that flared out at me. It was a world in which some things were elusive and uncertain, whilst other features loomed outwards, grabbing my attention.

I didn't sleep much. The ground was lumpy, matted with thin wiry grass that was also slippery against the fabric of my sleeping bag. I kept sliding downwards and waking up with a start a couple of yards away from where I'd laid down. I poked my head out the bag, gazed at the moon and peered at the lights of ships in the dim distance. A few drops of rain pattered loud on the fabric, and I listened out, expecting the start of a shower, but the drops slowed and silenced. I rolled about looking for a more comfortable spot but couldn't find one. I tried to sleep some more.

Nothing much happened. It was all rather uneventful and unremarkable, except that I obviously wasn't going to get much sleep that night. I lost track of time, though I could tell time was passing by the way the sea gradually sounded more distant with the outgoing tide. Eventually I thought it might be getting lighter. I dug my watch out of my pocket and, sure enough, it was 4am. I sat up, gave up on sleep, and stared into the darkness. There were a few bats flickering above me. From time to time gulls appeared overhead, seeming to just materialize out of the dark, ghostlike. I guess they were flying in from the sea, but they flew silently, just looming into view without me being able to see where they had come from. They were like spirit-birds coming from nowhere. If they saw me, they banked to one side with a kink of their wings, curving round me, making no call. I wondered about them, and whether they were cold or hungry.

Gradually it was getting lighter. The landmass to my right had been an amorphous grey, but was now a more distinct shape. Then I could distinguish fields from rock and cliff, and even make out the individual features of trees, hedges, and the little house. Birds began singing from behind me where there were a few small trees and scrubby undergrowth. I still had some water in my flask that was just about warm enough to brew a cup of tea. I sat and sipped the tea whilst that nocturnal world, in its turn, dissolved and gradually disappeared. Another world, another day, emerged out of the darkness. The photographic negative was transformed into a full-colour image. I watched as that scene gradually took its daytime shape again, and I listened to the languid chanting of the sea.

About 6am I began walking back home again; I was walking west with bright sunshine slanting down from behind me. Perhaps it was partly this angle of the sunlight, but everything seemed so utterly fresh, so completely pristine, as though rinsed clean in the night. Perhaps also my eyes, which had become adapted to night vision, focused just on making out basic shapes in light and dark, were now overwhelmed, bowled over, by the vividness of the colours. Each colour was as pure as if squeezed straight from a new tube of paint: the yellowest yellow flung from gorse blooms, intense saturated pink hurled from the campion flowers, vibrating green leaping from grass and leaves. The ocean was blue, blue and beautiful, or, in the shadow of the cliff, was a mysterious piscine silver-green.

Out of the quiet of night, the bustling hubbub of day was building. Jackdaws were already noisy and busy. Whitethroats collected food and took it back to nests hidden in the undergrowth. Out to sea a group of gannets were fishing. There would be a flash of white as one turned into a dive, then another flash, a spume of white spray, as the bird hit the water. I startled a copper-red fox and it scuttled off, skirting the edge of the field, until it bounded into the hedgerow. A seal poked its head out of the water and looked up at me, watching carefully.

As I walked through their field, a herd of mushroom-white cows mostly ignored me, though the straggle-coated ponies were more wary and watching. Then, coming up to a gate, I saw a small deer on the other side, dozing in the long grass, drowsy, enjoying the morning sun. The deer was the colours of autumn bracken, in parts pale-gold like the bleached stems of bracken, elsewhere the bronzy, russet-red of old leaves. It clambered to its feet when it saw me, looked at me, licked its nose, and didn't seem too bothered, just mildly curious. After a few minutes of us watching each other, I started to unfasten the gate. At the click of the latch the deer disappeared instantly into the dense thicket of gorse and blackthorn.

I felt joyful and happy; that strip of wildness was so beautiful. About 9am I arrived back into the little harbour town. Here a new day was also just getting going: nothing special or dramatic, just the humdrum, everyday routine. It was all so ordinary and familiar, yet I also felt a sense of 'return' as if I had been away for ages. But it was now time to come back home. It was time to return to the human world.

Now, as so many times before in the preceding twenty-five years, I was in the process of returning from solitary retreat. I knew I was going back to very different conditions in the city, and that they would inevitably affect me. It would be hard to sustain the aliveness and openness I found in nature once immersed in the urban environment. But I also knew that I didn't need to 'revert' entirely to who I had been before. Something of the wild open coastline would stay with me. I would return home more aware, more grounded and confident.

I walked through the streets down to the little harbour. Two builders were starting work on a scaffolded building. The shop was just opening, and a woman was wheeling a rack of postcards out onto the pavement. A van drew up with a food delivery for the pub next door. Three people chatted on the street corner. The ferryman was in a cheery mood as he carried his passenger over the river.

Appendix 1

An A-to-Z guide
to solitary retreats

Some readers of an early draft of the main chapters of this book suggested that some more practical guidance on how to approach solitary retreats, and different ways you can do them, could be helpful. So I have followed their advice. I have written it in the form of an 'A-to-Z guide', partly to break the material up and make it a bit more lively, but also to give you a choice about whether to read it all through in one go, or to choose the sections that seem most relevant to you. It assumes that most readers will be doing *Buddhist* solitary retreats. However, even if you are not a Buddhist, but you are drawn to spending some time alone, I hope you will find something here that is helpful. There is a lot more that could have been said about some of the topics covered, such as meditation, ritual, or thinking and reflecting. What follows is designed to at least help get you going, or, in the case of someone who has already done solitary retreats, to provide some extra inspiration and ideas. Sometimes, as shorthand for solitary retreats, I refer to them as 'solitaries'.

A for Arriving

Our first day, or first few days, will be for arriving. We can't switch instantly into retreat mode; we need to allow time for our energy to shift down a few gears. On that first day we can perhaps create a shrine, as a focus for our retreat and especially for our meditation. We might also do a ritual for 'dedicating' the space we are staying in and making conscious and explicit our intention in being there (see **R for Ritual**). I have included in the second appendix a version of a ritual recited in the Buddhist community I am part of (the Triratna Buddhist Community). This ritual is usually used in group situations, so I have adapted it slightly for use by one person alone on retreat.[39]

We can walk slowly round the place, saying hello, being aware of the life of things and of the creatures that dwell there. We can be aware that we have, in a sense, come into their space. We can even, if it feels meaningful to us, ask for their support, help, and protection. (There is an ancient Buddhist text known as the *Ratana Sutta* that does just this; in the second appendix I have incorporated some verses based on and adapted from this text.[40]) Tuning in to that world around us can help take us out of our old self, and open us out into a more bright and aware way of being.

You can't rush arriving; it has its own time, its own rhythm. There is a lovely image for how meditation works that is just as applicable to the process of being on retreat. It is an image of a container of water. The water is somewhat muddy and also, swirling about in the water, are bits of muck and grit. We may experience our minds like that when we first arrive – still flurried, cloudy, and cluttered by bits and pieces of the life we have left behind. If we wait patiently, however, the mud starts to settle and the water stops swirling, allowing the bits and pieces to drift to the bottom. We are left with a container of water that is much more pure and clear. But it takes time. It can't be rushed. Trying to rush the process would be like trying to make the water settle by putting a stick in and prodding and poking at the bits and pieces that are floating around. This just stirs everything back up again. As with meditation, much of the process of retreat is about waiting. Perhaps even 'waiting' isn't quite the right word, as it might imply *expectation*, looking at your watch wondering when something is due to happen. We are not waiting in that sense, but just sitting and settling, though with an open and actively aware mind.

We may have habitual physical stances that are the embodiments of our mental and emotional states: tensed-up shoulders or a posture that is always slightly leaning forwards, for example. When we start to arrive on retreat we may notice quite physical changes; our whole body may feel like a fist unfolding. Or we are like a fern unfurling, or a creature coming tentatively out of its habitual, protective shell. We are gradually arriving.

See also **S for Suitability** for advice on whether a solitary retreat is for you, **P for Preparing** to go on one, **B for Balance** for discussion of different structures and styles of retreat and how to get the right balance, and also **V for Venue** with information about where to go for a solitary retreat.

B for Balance

What kind of 'programme' should you have on a solitary retreat? Or should you have any set timetable at all? This section is about the balance between a more structured, directed approach, and one that is more spontaneous, loose, and open. What is the balance between meditation and ritual, study and reflection, and time for just sitting or going out walking?

There are different ways to do solitaries, different 'styles' if you like. This book is partly the story of my journey of discovery of solitary retreats and a particular way of doing them (one in which nature features strongly – see **N for Nature**). Over the years the way you do solitaries may develop and evolve. They can be more purely meditative, or more focused around study and reflection, or on reciting a Buddhist text, or even based around drawing or poetry. You might stay in a wild and remote place with very basic facilities, or you might be somewhere more 'mild' than 'wild'.

When you are new to the practice of solitary retreat it is probably good to go for something quite balanced, with a mix of meditation, some study, ritual, and time for doing nothing. Have something of a stretch and build up the amount of meditation you do. Don't get too busy on solitary retreat reading books, doing art, and exploring places. Don't fill in all your time with activity. But don't throw yourself in too far towards the deep end either, by trying to do too much meditation and having too much empty space. You will probably need to 'feed' yourself to some extent by having a good novel to read for the first few days, and then something to study and reflect on.

Should we follow a programme or should we follow our intuition and be more spontaneous? Again, when we are relatively new to solitaries, I would suggest a bit of both. Have something of a daily programme, though you can allow yourself to adapt it as you go along. But also have open spaces within that daily routine and pattern. We might also go with some ideas of what we want to do in meditation or study. It is good to have ideas and intentions that give you an element of direction, purpose, and engagement. But, at the same time, keep it open. Don't get too busy; don't have fixed goals or deadlines. Solitary retreats are a chance to live in a different mode, to function in a different way to life back home.

See **F for Friendship** for discussion of getting guidance from someone more experienced. Also see **M for Meditation**, **R for Ritual**, and **T for Thinking** for more ideas of what you do whilst on retreat.

C for Clocks

On many solitaries I have had the practice of hiding my clock or watch away, and doing without clock time. See chapter 3 in particular for a description of what that can be like. You don't *have* to do this; it is just a possible idea to play with!

The basic idea is to be more relaxed around clock time. Perhaps we can make use of the position of the sun and organic time, rather than the mechanical time of the clock. Maybe we can eat when we are hungry and sleep when we're tired, rather than when the clock says it is time to do these things. We just experiment with loosening up around clock time. This can be helpful in encouraging an attitude in which we don't *have* to be doing or achieving anything, or justifying and accounting for our time. The point is to help us make the shift into a less driven and utilitarian mode, into one that is more appreciative, 'being' rather than 'doing'.

Doing without a watch or clock can also show us how we measure ourselves by time. For example, we want to know how long we meditated for, as a long meditation is somehow a 'successful' one, showing us what a good Buddhist we are! Time can be seen as an aspect of the identity that we cling to. We obtain a certain sense of security from knowing the time.

Time can also be a mirror to our state of mind. We see that our sense of time alters as our state of mind changes. As the proverb says, time flies when we're having fun – when we're happy, time seems like quicksilver. But when we're bored, time drags slowly – a watched kettle never boils, as the saying goes. But also, sometimes, we can forget about time and our experience can be tinged, or more than tinged, with a sense of timelessness. When we are alone we are thrown back on ourselves, we are made more aware of our own thoughts and moods. This can help us to see how our experience is constructed in the mind. Looking at how our subjective experience of time changes, we see that this 'mind-made' nature of experience also includes something as fundamental as our time sense. We are not 'in' time; time is 'in' consciousness, it is part of the form our consciousness takes.[41]

Treat all this as an experiment. Solitary retreats are a chance to experiment, to play, to be curious about life and experience, to try something different. But don't completely lose track of time and forget to go home! This may cause unnecessary anxiety to friends and loved ones who are expecting you back by a certain date!

D for Distraction

Probably we will all experience states of restlessness and distraction during solitaries. For an extreme case, see **K for Knitting**. I have also known someone come back from a solitary retreat having, halfway through, been to the hairdresser to get a perm. It is true that the idea of a retreat is to come back home transformed, but not quite like that.

I have known men who are fanatical about football run into difficulty if their retreat coincides with an important match. They take a detour through the local village during their afternoon walk so they can pass the pub and glance through the window at the match on the screen. Just to see the score. Then they find themselves loitering around outside the pub staring through the window. Then the people inside are staring at them, so they feel uncomfortable loitering and go in...

I also know someone who went to extraordinary lengths to get the final score of matches, arranging for a friend living in a nearby retreat centre to leave messages on small pieces of paper that were hidden at the roots of a certain tree.

These are just some of the external manifestations of distraction. There can be inner distractions too – music that won't stop playing in our heads, absurd fantasies, or unnecessary worries. I have spent breakfasts on solitary retreat memorizing the bumf on the back of the soya-milk carton, found myself reading a book that was left at the venue by the last person there, without quite remembering how the book got into my hands and was opened, or spending meditations thinking up items of food that were running low, necessitating an emergency trip to the shops.

We are a bundle of energy, or energies. These energies have a forward momentum – they want to *move*. They also have their habitual outlets in our everyday life. There are channels down which they usually flow, many of which may be perfectly healthy and good, or at least harmless, and some that may be less so. However, when we've come away on retreat those usual outlets and channels aren't available. But our energy can't just *stop*. It has to go somewhere. This can be uncomfortable – physically, emotionally, and mentally – and we experience restlessness and anxiety, and then (subconsciously) we look for some kind of outlet for our energy, a displacement activity. We seek to distract ourselves from the discomfort of that ill-fitting energy.

Working with that energy is all part of the process: not blocking or supressing it, nor frittering it away, but trying, gradually, to find deeper channels. It is no use being wilful; we need a wise and gradual approach (see **G for Growth**). We will probably go through different phases throughout the whole retreat and may experience further ups and downs of mood and energy (see **U for Undulations**). Physical activity such as yoga, t'ai chi, or walking can help. See also **H for Hard Times** and **O for Offline**.

E for Ending (and Going Home)

It is important to end well. We might have had a day or two for arriving at the start, and we probably also need a day or two for ending. We might finish with a ritual, perhaps forming intentions or resolutions for our life back home, and recording these in our journal. Perhaps that ritual might include expressions of gratitude and appreciation for the retreat, for whatever or whoever has made it possible, even for the place that we have been dwelling in, and that has held us. (See **R for Ritual**.)

We begin easing off the meditation and are aware that soon we will be in a faster-moving, faster-talking environment, one with much more stimulation and distraction. We can't be too precious and hold too tightly to the feel and atmosphere of our retreat. It will change as conditions change, and we will need to let go. However, we can make the transition with sensitivity and awareness.

We may return from a retreat feeling buoyant and joyful, with a replenished sense of meaning and purpose. At other times it is harder going home. Our energy has to readjust in the opposite direction to when we arrived. There can be a freeing up of energy on retreat and, when we get back home, it can be hard to keep control of it. Old habits and emotions suddenly spring back into life, or even seem to have renewed vigour. The energy can even spill over into irritation or moodiness. It can feel disappointing. But it doesn't mean our retreat was wasted; it is all part of the process of change, and that change getting fully integrated into our whole life and being.

It is probably wise to be a bit careful about meeting a family member or friend at the place where we have been spending time alone, especially if it is someone who doesn't do retreats themselves. It may have become a very special, even 'sacred' place to us. But other people, who haven't been through a process like we just have, may not be able to understand what it means to us, and this might be quite jarring.

Likewise, if we are going home to meet family and friends who don't share our Buddhist ideas and practice, this may require a bit of care and understanding. They may not be able to appreciate that we are in somewhat of a different state, more bright and aware, but also open and sensitive. Going back into the hurly-burly of ordinary life and perhaps not feeling quite understood, we might find anxiety or annoyance arising. Then our family are surprised that, having had so much time off being 'spiritual', we should get irritated so quickly! It has got to be negotiated with patience, tact, and humour.

F for Friendship

Obviously the idea of a solitary retreat is to experience solitude. But we might have someone back home, someone with a bit more experience of solitaries than us, whom we contact once or twice during the retreat for guidance and perspective.

If you read **O for Offline** you will see that I am really concerned that we avoid the potential distractions and temptations of mobile phones and electronic devices on retreat. Therefore, if we want to be in touch with a friend or guide during the retreat, we need to find a practical arrangement that works, that doesn't expose us to those distractions and temptations, or mean that the rest of the world will start contacting us.

I am not definitely or unquestioningly advocating having a 'retreat mentor'. It is not something I do myself, though I know others who find it helpful. Talking with someone else about what is going on can help us gain clarity and perspective. Perhaps, on our own, our thinking can get somewhat stuck, and another person asking questions or making suggestions can jolt us out of a rut and get us moving forward again. Or we simply benefit from their experience and guidance.

G for Growth

The metaphor of growth is one of the most commonly encountered in the Buddhist tradition, as in the image of the lotus growing up through the mud, breaking the surface of the water, and blooming in all its glory. It is a very helpful metaphor to keep in mind.

Every plant does need certain conditions in which to thrive and grow healthily. It needs enough sunlight and water, enough shelter from the wind and certain nutrients in the soil. In this way, human beings are like plants. We also need certain supportive conditions; it would be very hard to grow without them.

We can't rush the growth of a plant. It is no use digging a seed up to see if it has germinated yet, or to examine how well the roots are developing. We can't prise a plant's leaves open in order to speed up spring. All we need to do is to remember to water it. After that we just have to leave the plant be. It will grow in its own time.

Every type of plant is different and it grows in its own way. Some grow fast, some grow slow. Some are naturally tall and straight, others more spreading and bushy. Some have big lush leaves, others tiny thin needles. We, too, have to grow in our own way, according to our own nature. We can't look at a big impressive tree over there and decide we are going to grow *exactly* like that. It is fine to be inspired by other people and their qualities, as long as we know that we need to grow in our own time and according to our own nature.

Plants grow completely silently. They don't make a great song and dance about it. Mostly it is very quiet and ordinary. It is the same with the process of retreats. There might be more decisive, dramatic moments where a new shoot breaks through the soil into the sunlight, or when a bud bursts into flower. But mostly it is quiet and ordinary; we are just trundling along, getting on with our practice.

When a plant grows, much of what is happening is invisible. It takes place underground. Roots are developing and spreading, growing stronger. Likewise with human growth: you don't always see it straight away. We might feel that nothing is happening as a result of our meditation, but it might just be taking place deep down where we don't notice. Just keep practising, and don't try to push it, or rush it. A plant grows seasonally: there will be spurts of fast growth, and there will be more dormant periods where not much seems to be changing, although, in actual fact, buds are fattening and sap is stirring. We, too, go through different phases in our growth.

So think of being on retreat as like gardening, or propagating. We are finding out the particular ways we grow and flourish. Whatever happens can be part of that learning process. Nothing (even the difficult experiences that seem like failures) need be wasted. Everything can be slung onto the compost heap and turned into something healthy and helpful. Don't waste the opportunity of being on retreat; at the same time don't necessarily expect a bumper crop of fruit straight away.

H for Hard Times

There have been days on solitary retreats that have been amongst the happiest and most memorable of my life. There have also been plenty of challenging times. Usually the hard times are, at bottom, about some aspect of myself, or some emotion, that I don't want to experience. An intense resistance can build up, and this is difficult and painful.

The resistance may manifest as restlessness, and an inability to focus or settle. It may also be experienced as a listless boredom, a feeling of emptiness and lethargy, even as a sense of despair and futility. I have a particular knot that occasionally tightens up in my right shoulder, like a brick that has somehow got stuck inside the muscle, and it is another sign of emotional conflict and tension. The more we practise things like meditation, going on retreat, and solitude, the more we will know the signs, the process, and how to be kind and patient with ourselves, keep relaxing, keep opening to our experience. The challenge is to stay with it and not avoid oneself. (See **D for Distraction**!)

There can also be fear. Even the young Gautama, before he found the way to enlightenment and became the Buddha, described encountering strong 'fear and dread' whilst meditating in the forest.[42] He had to train himself to not fear the fear, but to carry on walking if he was walking, sitting if he was sitting, meditating if he was meditating. Obviously this has to be done kindly and not wilfully. At the same time, we will need courage and determination. We may also want, or need, to talk to someone during a challenging phase; some people will have a mentor or friend on hand that they can contact if they need to. This is a particular approach to solitaries discussed under **F for Friendship**. For a little bit more about fear specifically in meditation, see **Y for Yogi**.

People vary. I am probably more temperamentally suited to solitary retreats and find them relatively easy. Other people may find them more of a challenge. But, if approached in the right spirit, they will still be richly rewarding.

I for Idleness

Whatever you do on solitary retreat, do lots of nothing. In chapter 8 I talk about this in terms of 'disciplined idleness'. Just sit, perhaps with a cup of tea, perhaps with a view out of the window, and do nothing. Doing nothing is maybe the most important thing we can do.

It is not always easy. We may find restlessness rising up within us. We may get bored, or feel lethargic and sleepy. This is all part of the process of our energy readjusting and finding a new rhythm. So it requires a certain 'discipline' in the sense of staying with it, keeping at it, without trying to push our energy and experience into some preordained shape.

'Doing nothing' isn't daydreaming or drifting – even though that can feel rather pleasant! There is a place for allowing associative thought and imagery in the mind, and also a place for more directed, purposeful reflection. For more on this, see **T for Thinking**.

J for Journal

On my first ever solitary retreat I started to write a journal, which was something I had never done before. Each day I wrote a page or so describing my general experience, what was going on in my meditation, what had caught my eye whilst out walking, what thoughts or memories had cropped up in my mind, what had taken place in my dreams. It was the beginning of a practice of journal keeping that I have continued to this day.

When I read back through old journals, much of it is rather subjective, or just of its time and not of much lasting interest. But some of it contains useful insights, or memories of beautiful places and significant times. If I hadn't had my old journals to browse through I probably couldn't have written this book.

I would encourage you to try keeping a journal on your retreat. It can be a way of recording and reflecting on what is happening and, in the process, making it more clear and objective to you. Over the duration of the retreat, you start to see the ups and downs of your mood, and maybe start to see certain patterns emerging.

K for Knitting

I know someone who got extremely restless on her solitary retreat. It got to a point where she just couldn't stand it anymore. She left the place where she was staying and made a trip to the nearest town. She searched high and low in every likely shop for some balls of wool, so she could do some knitting. But it was only a small rural town and there was no wool to be found. It was a desperate situation. What to do?

She went into one of the clothes shops and bought a jumper. She took it back to her retreat. She quickly unravelled it and rolled it into a ball of wool. Then she started to knit... a jumper.

This story is probably a case of **D for Distraction**; see also **H for Hard Times** and **Q for Quitting**.

L for Length

How long should a solitary retreat be? My advice would be to slowly build it up, starting with something you feel comfortable with. This might be a long weekend or a few days. Then, next time, you might do five days or a week. Once you are more experienced you might want to work up to two or three weeks, or even a month.

Some people do even longer retreats, lasting several months or even years. Often they come back to 'the human world' with an energy and momentum of practice that sustains them for a long time. They are also able to share their inspiration so that other people benefit.

But our circumstances vary. Some people have worldly responsibilities and cannot get away for long periods of time. Do what you are able to do. Even in a day or two you can dip into something deep and precious. And maybe one day in the future you will have the opportunity to try for longer.

M for Meditation

In the main part of this book I haven't said that much specifically about meditation. I focused more on other aspects of being on solitary retreats and especially on how nature and sense of place came to matter so much to me, and to be such an intrinsic part of my approach.

But meditation has also been a crucial ingredient to those solitaries. Typically, I will start with two or three meditations per day, and then build it up so that eventually I am meditating for six or seven hours per day. There aren't rules about this, and it is not an endurance test or a competition. However, there can be a benefit in going for a stretch and seeing what happens.

On solitary retreat we are thrown back on our own resources in a particularly pure and uncompromising way. We see how our moods go up and down and we can no longer pin this on other people or circumstances. We see plainly that it is the ups and downs of our own mind. We see more clearly how what we do with our mind creates our world, our experience. Meditation is also, at least in part, about seeing just how fundamentally our experience is mind-created. So, in a way, we could say that a solitary retreat is like a long meditation, and a meditation is like a short retreat. For more on the process of meditation, see **G for Growth** and **Y for Yogi** (including some advice in case you encounter fear in meditation).

One last suggestion: it can be really good to do plenty of *metta bhavana* (loving-kindness meditation)[43] for all the people in our life back home. Sometimes on solitary retreat I feel very aware of people and appreciative of them. The time and space of a retreat give us a different perspective on how we tend to relate to them. It might seem paradoxical, but by being alone we can actually become *more* aware of our relatedness to others, and of our love for them. For more on this, see chapter 7.

N for Nature

For me, an integral part of being on solitary retreat is my relationship with the place and with the creatures that live there. On some solitaries my heart has opened, and I have felt connected to the world like never before. Places have their own character and atmosphere, and they can speak to us, or gesture to us. Our inner world and the outer world can communicate with one another.

For that reason, I seek out places that are wild and remote, around which I can go roaming and exploring. But I would say that awareness of our surroundings is part of any solitary retreat. Even if you are staying somewhere less wild and remote, nearer human habitation or on more cultivated and worked land, the place will still have a particular personality and mood. There will still be season, weather, day and night. There will still be a particular dance of earth and rain, wind and sun, a distinctive ecology of trees and plants and creatures. If you listen to those places, they will still speak with you.

Some people who read an earlier version of this book were friends of mine who didn't know so much about nature – in the sense of knowing the names of different species of birds or plants, and so on. They told me that some advice about how to learn to appreciate nature would be helpful. Where do you start, given that there are hundreds of different types of birds, flowers, or butterflies?

There are whole books written on this topic and on nature as a 'spiritual practice'.[44] But, for now, here are just a few suggestions to get you started.

Firstly, and centrally, it is about the senses. Look, listen, touch, smell. Look in close at the 'minute particulars' of things: the five spots on the inside of every cowslip flower, the chest-puffed-out gait and mannerisms of the little robin, the tropical smell of gorse blossom, the cold and wet of dewy grass under your bare feet, the scratchy sound of wind on dry beech leaves. Then look out far and wide, take in the whole scene, the whole landscape and soundscape. Observe. This will gradually draw out and broaden your awareness; it will gently expand and refine your consciousness.

You might choose a particular spot you go to everyday (or more often). Simply sit there for twenty minutes (or longer), watching and listening. Another approach to take would be to walk very slowly for (say) 500 steps. Notice what you notice on the way, and when you get to the 500th step just stop there and see where you have arrived and what that place says to you. You might take a pen and notepad with you, and write down what you experience.

What about learning the names of trees, flowers, and birds? Some people are of the opinion that this creates a veneer of words and labels, removing us one layer from the here and now, and preventing us from fully appreciating what is around us. But I don't quite agree with that. Of course we can end up identifying plants or birds in a 'tick box' kind of way, but knowing one species from another doesn't inevitably mean we take that approach. Actually, a bit more knowledge helps us know what to look for. We can understand more of the diversity and variety of what is out there. It can help us tune in more vividly and sensitively to the way a robin is different from a dunnock, or a wagtail from a dipper. So you could, for example, buy a good bird book and learn a few of the birds that you see (though I wouldn't recommend turning a solitary retreat into too much of an ornithological field trip). And it is also true that we don't need to know the names of things to observe and enjoy them, and to notice their personality and behaviour.

O for Offline

This section is about electronic gadgets: phones, devices, computers, or any technology for connecting to the internet, or the phone network, or even radio and TV. I want to strongly advocate that you go completely 'offline' whilst you are on retreat.

These days, this is a really vital issue. I remember when mobile phones first became common. It was during a phase of my life when I was leading lots of group retreats, and I watched what happened. Once upon a time, in the days before mobile phones, people just came on retreat and were able to leave their daily life behind them. But once mobile phones became ubiquitous, then people arrived on retreat and needed to phone home to let their family know they'd arrived, then phoned back fifteen minutes later to remind them to feed the cat, then phoned the office to say they would deal with that query on Monday, and then worried about what would happen if there was an emergency and the mobile-phone signal wasn't strong enough in the countryside for a message to get through. It seemed to me that, as well as allowing ease of communication, mobile-phone technology also allowed a whole load of fussing and fidgeting, a mass of anxiety *that simply wasn't possible before*. By all means make use of technology in your life. But don't let it use you and take you over.

We think technology gives us freedom and flexibility. And in some ways it does. But, at exactly the same time, it traps and confines us. For example, I know self-employed people who say they cannot go on retreat without checking their phone every day, as these days their customers expect an instantaneous reply. Once upon a time this was not an issue for them. They used to be able to forget about work for a few days and be on retreat carefree. Now they are slaves to their business. Yes, technology gives us power. But it also has power over us.

I know a retreat centre where they have had to take a hard line on this, insisting that people who attend retreats don't bring electronic gadgets. They tell people who don't feel able to do this not to come on retreat. These days this is very radical, even controversial! The team at the retreat centre felt it was vital they made a stand on this because the retreat atmosphere was being compromised by people constantly checking texts, or keeping others in their dormitory awake downloading films and music from under their duvet. There were a couple of more serious disruptions when retreats happened to coincide with important political elections going on in the world outside. Some people on the retreat had said they didn't want to hear the results of the elections; they just wanted to be on retreat undistracted, and they would find out the result when they got home. But other people on the retreat just could not stop themselves going online and finding out what had happened. And then, of course, they could not stop themselves from talking about it. The result was that a special atmosphere, that had taken days to create and build up, was totally spoilt.

If we spend our solitary retreat fiddling with our phone or sending the odd text, it may seem harmless enough. We may not notice the effect it is having on us. But it inhibits our ability to be fully present. We stay shallow, skimming over the surface of life. We are missing out on the opportunity to let go of daily concerns and sink into something deeper.

We tell ourselves, 'I'll bring my phone but leave it in flight mode.' We might say, 'I need my phone because I use it as an alarm clock.' We worry that, 'I want to be able to contact my family in an emergency.' But if you take that phone with you, will you truly be able to resist the temptation to go online or to check your messages? Here is what to do if you are worried about emergency situations. If the venue has a landline, give that number to one person and tell them it is strictly for emergencies. Otherwise, buy a cheap, pay-as-you-go mobile, and give that number to one person and tell them the same thing. Then go completely offline. Allow yourself to be really, truly, completely alone.

P for Preparing

We have already looked at the process of arriving on retreat (see **A for Arriving**). But it is good to begin preparing before we even turn up at the venue. My main point here is to do all we can to make practical arrangements at home and work so that we can properly leave when it is time to leave, and we are not still trying to tie up loose ends during our first days on retreat. Be smart about it. Plan ahead so that you can arrive wherever you are staying having put those worldly concerns down, and able to feel free and unencumbered.

Q for Quitting

I have known people quit part-way through a solitary retreat, or cut it short towards the end. Perhaps it just gets too intense, too lonely, or the restlessness is too much to cope with, or difficult emotions have arisen. Or maybe we have tried, done our best, definitely given ourselves a stretch and challenge, but now it feels like enough is enough and we don't want to push it.

There is a case for having a friend or guide that we can contact and talk to, especially if we are having a very difficult time, or thinking of leaving the retreat. Talking to someone might take the pressure off and show us a way forward. For discussion of this, see **F for Friendship** and also **H for Hard Times**.

Of course it is good to stay the course if we can. But if we can't, it is OK. It can feel a bit humiliating, but it happens. Solitaries are not an endurance test. Whatever has happened during our time there, we can learn from it. Whatever we learn will be valuable and contribute to a more mature and experienced understanding of who and what we are, and how our mind works. Whatever positive effort we made during our time there will have made a difference and won't be wasted.

R for Ritual

During a solitary retreat we might do traditional Buddhist rituals (puja), and we might bring along favourite readings or poems to read. A solitary retreat can also provide an ideal opportunity to engage with a longer Buddhist sutra or text, perhaps by reading it aloud for an hour or two each day. In the space of a retreat we may become more receptive and be able to enter the world, and particular atmosphere, of those texts much more fully than when we try reading them at home.

Often Buddhist ritual is done with other people, as a communal practice. It is a different experience doing it alone, but it can still be effective. When doing a ritual by myself I sometimes imagine other people also performing the ritual at different times and places, so that I am not so alone in my imagination, and feel connected to the wider sangha, or community.

We might also devise our own rituals to mark the start and the end of the retreat, or to help make conscious and heartfelt our intentions and aspirations. Ritual can be done indoors, and it is good to do ritual outside too. I know people who recite pujas whilst walking slowly along, or who recite different verses of a ritual at different places along their walk. This might sound strange to you now, but once you are on retreat and immersed in the wild world, it might feel much more natural.

Ritual is the outward expression, or enactment, of an inner change or emotional transformation. That outward embodiment can help make what is going on clearer and more explicit; expressing something actually helps brings it forth into fullness and completion. Ritual can help bring out emotions of joy and gratitude, or sadness and grief, regret and remorse, or determination and dedication.

Rituals need a 'content' and a 'form' that is appropriate and suitable for that content. By 'content' I mean what it is that you are trying to express; the 'form' is the particular words and actions with which you do that. Sometimes you see people doing ritual that is all form and no content; there are candles and light, drums and noise, but it isn't clear what the point of it is. At other times there is a well-meaning purpose, but the form isn't beautiful or adequate enough to express it. To be meaningful, a ritual needs a harmony of form and content.

To give an obvious example: if you became aware of regrets from the past that you wanted to confess, acknowledge, and put behind you, then that would be the 'content', or the purpose of your ritual. You might then choose to write down the confessions on paper, to recite some verses to the Buddha, and then set light to the piece of paper – so that the confessions burn in the fires of transformation and you are set free. That is the 'form', the outward words and actions that express and help reinforce the inner process and aspiration.

S for Suitability

Who are solitaries for? Would it be a good idea for you to do a solitary retreat? Probably it is advisable to do at least one guided group retreat first, to get an idea of how a retreat works, the inner process you go through on retreat and how to work with that. It is also a good idea to ask Buddhist friends if they think you having extended time alone seems sensible and appropriate.

If you are someone who needs a lot of structure and finds it difficult to be self-motivated, then solitaries are going to be challenging! Maybe an organized group retreat will be better for you. If you have mental-health issues, then you should get advice before going off spending a lot of time on your own.

The young man who would one day become the Buddha went into the forest to meditate, and he experienced fear. But he was able to stay with the fear and, eventually, transform it. Later on, when he was asked how he was able to do this, and why being in the dark and dangerous forest didn't 'rob him of his mind', he replied that it was because he had a pure ethical practice.

If big ethical issues have been part of our life, then we need to be aware that emotions and drives connected with these may manifest in the open space of a retreat. For example, if we've been involved in intense conflict, then anger and negative emotion may crop up. If we have lived a life of strong cravings and addictions, then these may also arise on retreat. Are we ready for that? If we have acknowledged unskilfulness from the past and are trying to put it behind us, then being on retreat may help. But if there is unacknowledged unskilfulness, or unethical behaviour that we are still engaging in, then this may come and confront us, which can be very challenging.

But I don't want to put anyone off trying solitude! Even if we have a difficult time, even if we leave early, we can still learn so much (see **Q for Quitting**). Solitary retreats are such a good opportunity to experience ourselves more deeply and fully. And, even if we find some shadow and darkness, that won't be all we find. There is only shadow because, beyond that, there is also light. Behind the dark clouds is dazzling brightness.

T for Thinking

On my first ever solitary retreat the experience of not talking to anyone for days and weeks was a real novelty. I describe some of what happened in chapter 1. Such silence can be unfamiliar, perhaps even a touch unnerving. Maybe what we notice at first is the voice inside our head incessantly talking. Because it is quiet 'outside', we become more aware of the 'noise within'. But then, in time, even that voice softens and hushes, and becomes less driven and urgent. There are more pauses, more moments of silence, which can be a huge relief. We may also notice how much energy usually goes into talking and listening to others talking, because in silence that energy is freed up and we feel it bubbling up inside us. So, whilst alone, savour that silence.

Space and silence can help create the conditions for more fruitful thinking and reflecting. When I have talked elsewhere in the book about 'idleness' or 'doing nothing', I mean by this just sitting – not trying to do anything, achieve anything, or solve any problems, but just staying aware and present in the experience of sitting there. But we will also have the opportunity to sit and think, or walk and think: to reflect on our experience, to turn over some topic or teaching that we want to understand more deeply, to consider carefully how it relates to our life and experience. Make time for thinking and reflecting.

How do you reflect? This is a big topic and all there is space for here is a few comments.[45] Reflection is a whole 'art' or practice in itself. We all know how our thoughts can often have a mind of their own, and it can be hard to think clearly and creatively. When we try to direct our thoughts to an issue, they suddenly dry up, we feel tired and lethargic, or we can't seem to focus. But with practice we can learn to reflect.

I often reflect by sitting with pencil and paper and doing one of those 'spider diagrams' where you write the topic in the middle of the page and then, around that, jot down ideas and points as they occur to you, and make connections between them with arrows and lines. I like to use pencil and paper because it helps give my thinking more focus and also, obviously, it means I end up with a written record of what came to mind.

Thinking can be a mysterious process. We will all have had the experience of thinking about a problem or issue and only managing to get so far; we are left feeling we haven't yet got to the bottom of the matter. But then, a few days later, interesting thoughts and ideas suddenly appear out of thin air. They burst into consciousness and we have no idea where they sprang from. It is like another department of our mind has been thinking about it all the while.

Sometimes we want to think in a more definite, focused, directed fashion. There is also a place for more free and associative thinking. By 'associative' I don't mean just mental chatter, the mind on autopilot, darting hither and thither, or just vaguely drifting. As Sangharakshita suggests:

you have to keep an eye on the direction your thought is
moving so that your associative thinking takes place within
a broader sense of purpose [...] It is still directed thinking
in a sense, although it is being directed from a distance [...]
All your thinking should have an aim, even if that aim is
sometimes best served by thinking associatively.[46]

U for Undulations

Any retreat will have a rhythm; it goes through undulations and
phases. You get to know the way it works for you. Sometimes I
have alternate 'easy' and 'difficult' days. One day feels smooth
and pleasant, but this allows some new emotion or energy to
come into consciousness, and then the next day is more rough
and bumpy as I work in meditation to integrate it.

We learn to see the ups and downs as part of the process. The
'downs' aren't necessarily signs of failure, or of doing the wrong
thing. Quite the contrary; they can often be an indication that we
are getting deeper. One of the most famous songs of the Tibetan
yogi Milarepa was his 'Song of a Yogi's Joy' in which he sang: 'The
more ups-and-downs I feel, the more joy I feel.'[47] Experiencing
stronger ups and downs tells him that he is freeing up deeper
emotions and energies, and that makes him even more happy
and joyful.

There is no right or wrong pattern; we just vary in temperament.
With some people it is smooth, quiet, and easy – or at least it
appears that way from the outside. With others it looks more
bumpy, stormy, and difficult. But in both cases something useful
and creative might be going on.

An analogy I find useful is that of an aeroplane wing.[48] If
you look at a cross section of the wing, it has a 'leading edge'
that faces the front and cuts through the air, and then a 'trailing
edge' at the back of the wing, which follows behind. We are like

that wing. We have a leading edge of our deepest experiences and understandings. But, usually, these are not fully integrated. Though that leading edge represents something genuine and valuable, not all of our behaviour is congruent with it yet. We are not consistently living at our best; those insights and deeper perspectives come and go. There is a trailing edge still with catching up to do.

With some people, probably the majority, the trailing edge is not that far behind the leading edge. These kinds of people tend to proceed at a fairly consistent pace without too much turbulence; it is all pretty stable and steady. For other people, the leading edge flies at supersonic speed, but the trailing edge lags way behind. The leading edge is fast and impressive looking, but the whole thing is much less stable and there tends to be more turbulence. Again, it is not that one of these is better than the other; it is a question of temperament. We are the type that we are. Whichever we are, we just need to get on with our practice.

V for Venue

Where do we go for a solitary retreat? The essential ingredients are somewhere quiet where we can be alone and undisturbed, somewhere simple and uncluttered and conducive to meditation, and somewhere 'offline'.

Some retreat centres have facilities for people to go and do solitary retreats. These can be very good, perhaps especially if we are new to solitaries. Or if you feel unsafe being alone in an isolated place then this is a good option, as there will be people around you, though they will also understand why you are there and keep your space undisturbed. Such places should be set up with the facilities you need. Some places will even provide food and provisions, so you don't need to go shopping.

It can be hard to find good places to do retreats. Dwellings in beautiful places tend to get converted into luxury holiday cottages with broadband, TV, and other facilities you don't want, at a price you can't afford. I feel very grateful to the people who have made available the places I have stayed in, the places described in this book. But, luckily, those places do exist and if you ask around in Buddhist circles then you can find out about them.

W for Wildness

Breathe deep into that buffeting wind. Don't hunch up against the weather, but let the raindrops sting the skin of your face. Walk barefoot and feel the ooze of the sodden earth under your feet. Don't go for comfort, go for wildness. You don't necessarily need to be in remote wilderness to do this: the elements of earth, water, fire, and air are dancing about you right now.

X for X Factor

The x factor, as they say, is the sex factor. On retreat it is a good idea to abstain from sexual activity, both bodily and mentally. Experience may obviously vary according to gender, and for people of different ages, but it could be said that a lot of our sexual craving is due to our emotional energy looking for a quick and easy outlet. When our life isn't emotionally satisfying and meaningful, then, in those moments of boredom, frustration, dullness, and emptiness, the mind can easily turn to sexual craving and fantasy.

On retreat there hopefully is more meaning and emotional fulfilment. Consequently, the mind may turn to sexual craving less often, and we naturally experience more contentment. This can be a big relief. Any desire that is still present can feel more 'natural' in the sense that it is just the normal sexual urge, quite human and healthy. It might feel more purely physical, located more in the *body*, in contrast to the sexual craving of the city that can be more of a fantasy in the *head*.

However, if it has become a habit, then craving won't simply stop just because we are now on retreat. Consequently, there may still be times when craving arises; it may even be very strong and prevalent. One way we can work with this is to practise 'unhooking'. We try to be aware of the body and the feeling of the desire in the body. Can we feel the underlying drive and energy, rather than being drawn into the fantasy or image that has become the object of that drive and energy? We unhook the energy from the fantasy and see that it is just energy. It isn't inherently 'bad' or 'good' in itself; it is energy that can take a myriad of different forms. If we stay practising in this way, it can be surprising how quickly the energy can change, and a fantasy that seemed so urgent and pressing just dissolves away into nothing.

We can also look for interest, enjoyment, and contentment in other areas of our experience, as a way of countering the tendency to craving. In other words, we are not trying to block the energy, but find it somewhere more truly satisfying to go. Watching and enjoying the breath in meditation, observing what is outside the window as we sit drinking our cup of tea, we can gradually refine our awareness. Solitary retreats can be a precious opportunity to experience a deeper happiness and contentment.

Y for Yogi

The main entry on meditation is under **M for Meditation** and there are also a few ideas about how the process of meditation works under **G for Growth**. This entry is about how to relate to unusual experiences that may (or may not) occur when we meditate.

'Bliss bunny' is an affectionate term for those people who seem quite easily and spontaneously to get into deeply tranquil, peaceful, and concentrated meditative states. Some people do take to meditation like a duck to water. They are natural yogis, and seem to have a facility for becoming very absorbed and focused, just like other people might have a facility for drawing, or remembering facts, or falling into conversation with strangers easily, or finding ingeniously simple ways to fix something mechanical. For some of us, it's the meditative faculty that seems to come easily and naturally.

Here are just a couple of points to bear in mind. If you are something of a bliss bunny (and of course the rest of us aren't jealous), then don't forget to stay grounded in the body. Allow releases of energy and a sense of deepening and expanding of consciousness, but also come back at the end of meditation to feeling your backside on the cushion and your feet and legs on the floor. Allow time to integrate whatever has happened.

If you are not a bliss bunny and you find meditation more like hard work, then don't worry. It doesn't mean you aren't a 'good meditator'. Meditation is about changing, gradually becoming more aware and kind, not necessarily about having special experiences in meditation. Just take meditation at your own pace, work steadily, and keep it creative.

Sometimes we encounter fear in meditation. Perhaps we go deeper into meditation than we have done before, and our awareness and sense of ourselves starts to feel quite different. When this is unfamiliar it can be disconcerting, or even frightening. If this happens to you, try working at that 'edge'. If what is happening seems too strange, then you can 'back off' a bit, ground yourself in awareness of the physical body, feel your breath, and take it at your own pace. Perhaps, after a while, you can try to move deeper into the meditation again and see if what is occurring now feels more familiar and safe. Remember to do lots of body awareness and also *metta bhavana* (loving-kindness meditation). If we do this, and as long as we are not forcing anything, then we will be OK. This is an area of practice where having someone to check in with can be beneficial, especially someone with experience of meditation (see **F for Friendship**).

Z for ZZZ

Z is for ZZZ, for sleep and dreams. Sometimes I have kept a 'dream diary' whilst on solitary retreat. I just keep a pencil and notebook by the bedside and, as soon as I wake in the morning, I record as much as I can remember about my dreams. The first day or two I am only able to jot down odd fragments. A few days later, and I'm able to recall quite a number of dreams. If I keep at it, then, eventually, I find myself writing pages and pages and still not getting everything down that I can remember.

Personally, I don't try too hard to analyze the dreams. Often I think people try to force an interpretation, or do it in a rather textbook, if-you-dream-about-X-then-it-means-Y, manner. However, it is interesting and revealing to see what themes, characters, or emotions recur and resurface. Perhaps occasionally we have a very strong dream that feels significant, and we can immediately intuit its meaning. In dreams it can seem like our usual, relatively superficial, ego-self is no longer in control and other aspects of our mind are able to express themselves. The dream world is more fluid, more associative and non-literal.

It is as if we live in several worlds at once, or different realms within the one world of experience. Those worlds and realms are all interconnected. There is the beautiful world of nature and the other forms of life around us, the flickering world of our waking thoughts and inner conversations, the more radiant world of meditation and imagination, and the underworld of dreams. Maybe we usually, habitually, live predominantly in the second of these worlds, but on retreat they can all become more vivid, alive, and overlapping. Why live only in one world when you can live in four? Why not live a life of awareness, live life more fully in *all* its dimensions?

Appendix 2

Two ritual texts for being alone and aware in nature

Dedication ceremony (adapted from the Triratna dedication ceremony)[49]

> I dedicate this place to the Three Jewels:
> To the Buddha, the ideal of enlightenment to which I aspire;
> To the Dharma, the path of the teaching which I follow;
> To the Sangha, the spiritual community to which I belong.
>
> Here may I dwell without distraction;
> Here may no unquiet thought disturb my mind.
>
> To the observance of the five precepts
> I dedicate this place;
> To the practice of meditation
> I dedicate this place;
> To the development of wisdom
> I dedicate this place;
> To the attainment of enlightenment
> I dedicate this place.
>
> Though in the world outside there is strife
> Here may there be peace;

Two ritual texts for being alone and aware in nature

Though in the world outside there is hate
Here may there be love;
Though in the world outside there is grief
Here may there be joy.

Not by the chanting of the sacred scriptures,
Not by the sprinkling of holy water,
But by my own efforts towards enlightenment
I dedicate this place.

Around this mandala, this sacred spot,
May the lotus petals of purity open;
Around this mandala, this sacred spot,
May the vajra-wall of determination extend;
Around this mandala, this sacred spot,
May the flames that transmute samsara into nirvana arise.

Here seated, here practising,
May my mind become Buddha,
May my thought become Dharma,
May my heart be in harmony with the Sangha.

For the happiness of all beings,
For the benefit of all beings,
With body, speech, and mind,
I dedicate this place.

'Whatever beings are gathered here...'
(adapted from the *Ratana Sutta*)[50]

Whatever beings are gathered here,
Whether of the earth, water, or air,
May you all be well and happy,
May you know that I come in peace.

Please listen carefully to what I say,
Please accept these offerings of mine,
And send your loving-kindness towards the human race.

Whatever beings are gathered here,
Whether of the earth, water, or air,
Let us pay homage to the Buddha,
And by this act may there be peace!

Whatever beings are gathered here,
Whether of the earth, water, or air,
Let us pay homage to the Dharma,
And by this act may there be peace!

Whatever beings are gathered here,
Whether of the earth, water, or air,
Let us pay homage to the Sangha,
And by this act may there be peace!

Whatever beings are gathered here,
Whether of the earth, water, or air,
May you all be well and happy,
May you know that I come in peace.

Notes

1 Henry David Thoreau, *Walden: or, Life in the Woods*, Dover Publications, New York 1995, p.136.

2 Local Welsh people were sometimes unable to afford housing because they'd been priced out of the market by wealthier English people moving in or buying second homes in the area.

3 Buddhism was founded by the Buddha, a historical figure who lived about 2,500 years ago in what is now northern India. But in the Buddhist tradition there are many different, more mythical and archetypal, Buddha figures. Each will have its own symbolism and iconography and embody a different quality of the enlightened mind.

4 Nan Shepherd, *The Living Mountain*, in *The Grampian Quartet*, Canongate, Edinburgh 1996, p.79.

5 Thoreau, *Walden*, p.58.

6 Ted Hughes, *Moortown Diary*, Faber and Faber, London 1989, p.19.

7 David Abram, *The Spell of the Sensuous*, Vintage, New York 1997, p.49.

8 Quoted in Gordon Haight, *George Eliot: A Biography*, Penguin, New York 1985, p.201.

9 Whilst writing this I came across the following quote from the pioneering conservationist and nature writer John Muir:

Notes# *Notes*

'I only went out for a walk, and finally concluded to stay out till sundown, for going out, I found, was really going in.' It is quoted in Robert Macfarlane, *Wild Places*, Granta, London 2008, underneath the dedication of the book.

10 Sangharakshita, *The Yogi's Joy: Songs of Milarepa*, Windhorse Publications, Birmingham 2006, p.186.

11 Richard Louv, *Last Child in the Woods: Saving Our Children from Nature-Deficit Disorder*, Atlantic Books, London 2010, pp.74 and 100.

12 See http://en.wikipedia.org/wiki/The_Nightingale_%28fairy_tale%29, accessed on 18 August 2017.

13 Dharmashakya, 'Awareness of nature', a talk given at the London Buddhist Centre in 2014 and available at https://www.freebuddhistaudio.com/audio/details?num=LOC2047, accessed on 18 August 2017.

14 See, for example, Anthony Storr, *Solitude*, Collins, London 1989.

15 Thoreau, *Walden*, p.59.

16 D.H. Lawrence, 'Snake', in *Birds, Beasts, and Flowers*, Penguin, London 1999, p.99.

17 Storr, *Solitude*, p.62.

18 *Udana* 2.1, in *The Udana and the Itivuttaka*, trans. John D. Ireland, Buddhist Publication Society, Kandy 1997, p.23.

19 It is also interesting to note that in biblical mythology it is a serpent that slyly encourages Adam and Eve to eat the fruit of the Tree of Knowledge, and so fall into separation from nature. In Buddhist mythology, it is a snake that helps and protects the Buddha as he overcomes human pride and alienation and is reunited with nature.

20 Thomas A. Clark, 'Five waves', 2003, a five-line poem available as a postcard from Essence Press at https://www.juliejohnstone.com/essence-press/, accessed on 18 August 2017.

21 Robert Hass, *The Essential Haiku: Versions of Basho, Buson, and Issa*, Bloodaxe Books, Tarset 2013, p.35.

22 Shepherd, *The Living Mountain*, p.49.

Notes

23 Ted Hughes, *Collected Poems*, Farrar, Straus and Giroux, New York 2003, p.315.

24 J.A. Baker, *The Peregrine*, HarperCollins, London 2010.

25 Baker, *The Peregrine*, p.125.

26 Quoted in Jonathan Bate, *John Clare: A Biography*, Picador, London 2004, p.276.

27 Peter Redgrove, *The Black Goddess and the Sixth Sense*, Paladin, London 1989.

28 One example that I once heard of is that of the South Pacific Islanders, who, hundreds of years ago, were able to navigate thousands of miles across the ocean without compasses or instruments. It is said that they could pick up signs of currents and tides, and from that work out where land was likely to lie, by dipping the palms of their hands into the water.

29 Macfarlane, *Wild Places*, p.193, see also pp.201–2.

30 Louis MacNeice, 'Snow', in *Collected Poems*, Faber and Faber, London 2002, p.30.

31 Ted Hughes, *Poetry in the Making: A Handbook for Writing*, Faber and Faber, London 2008, pp.18–19.

32 Baker, *The Peregrine*, pp.35–6.

33 Ted Hughes, *The Hawk in the Rain*, Faber and Faber, London 1986, p.11.

34 Frédéric Gros, *A Philosophy of Walking*, Verso, London 2014, p.99.

35 *Udana* 4.5, in *The Udana and the Itivuttaka*, trans. Ireland, p.58.

36 See Vishvapani Blomfield, *Gautama Buddha: The Life and Teachings of the Awakened One*, Quercus, London 2011, p.182ff. In addition, P.D. Ryan, *Buddhism and the Natural World: Towards a Meaningful Myth*, Windhorse Publications, Birmingham 1998, contains a wealth of information and stories about the experience of the natural world of the Buddha and his followers.

37 The painting, *The Buddha in the Forest*, by Alan Shipway, is reproduced in Wendy Beckett, *Art and the Sacred*, Rider, London 1992, p.132.

38 The elephant was called Nalagiri and the story is found in the *Cullavagga*; see *The Book of the Discipline (Vinaya Pitaka)*, vol.5, trans. I.B. Horner, Pali Text Society, Oxford 1992, section 7, pp.272–4. You might ask how much of the story is fact and how much is legend. But it may not be too far-fetched to be true. There are many records of monks meditating in forests, having close encounters with elephants and tigers, and living to tell the tale. See, for example, Kamala Tiyavanich, *Forest Recollections: Wandering Monks in Twentieth-Century Thailand*, University of Hawai'i Press, Honolulu 1997.

39 The original Triratna dedication ceremony can be found in Sangharakshita, *Puja: The Triratna Book of Devotional Texts*, Windhorse Publications, Cambridge 2008, p.36.

40 You can find translations of the complete text of the *Ratana Sutta* at http://accesstoinsight.org, accessed on 18 August 2017.

41 For more on time and timelessness, see my forthcoming book, *Free Time*.

42 This story is told in the *Bhayabherava Sutta* in the *Majjhima Nikaya*, trans. Bhikkhu Nanamoli and Bhikkhu Bodhi, Wisdom Publications, Somerville, MA 2005, pp.102–7.

43 The *metta bhavana* is a particular meditation practice in which we cultivate *metta*, or loving-kindness, towards ourselves and other people.

44 The best book I have come across on nature appreciation as a practice is Mark Coleman, *Awake in the Wild: Mindfulness in Nature as a Path of Self-Discovery*, New World Library, Novato, CA 2006.

45 For much more on this topic, see Ratnaguna, *The Art of Reflection*, Windhorse Publications, Cambridge 2010. Chapter 12 of Sangharakshita, *Living with Awareness: A Guide to the Satipatthana Sutta*, Windhorse Publications, Birmingham 2003, is also very good on thought and thinking.

46 Sangharakshita, *Living with Awareness*, p.119.

47 *The Hundred Thousand Songs of Milarepa*, trans. Garma C.C. Chang, Shambhala Publications, Boston 1999, p.75.

48 Thanks to Vajrapriya for this image!

49 See note 39. The symbolism and imagery of the dedication ceremony are based around the creation of a mandala (a sacred and protective circle). Outside that circle is the human world with its strife, hate, and grief; inside the circle you dedicate the space (and yourself) to the Three Jewels, and to practising ethics, meditation, and wisdom.

50 See note 40.

Bibliography

Abram, David, *Becoming Animal: An Earthly Cosmology*, Vintage, New York 2011.

Abram, David, *The Spell of the Sensuous*, Vintage, New York 1997.

Ansell, Neil, *Deep Country: Five Years in the Welsh Hills*, Penguin, London 2012.

Baker, J.A., *The Peregrine*, HarperCollins, London 2010.

Batchelor, Stephen, *Alone with Others: An Existential Approach to Buddhism*, Grove Press, New York 1983.

Bate, Jonathan, *John Clare: A Biography*, Picador, London 2004.

Bate, Jonathan, *The Song of the Earth*, Picador, London 2001.

Beckett, Wendy, *Art and the Sacred*, Rider, London 1992.

Blomfield, Vishvapani, *Gautama Buddha: The Life and Teachings of the Awakened One*, Quercus, London 2011.

Chang, Garma C.C., trans., *The Hundred Thousand Songs of Milarepa*, Shambhala Publications, Boston 1999.

Coleman, Mark, *Awake in the Wild: Mindfulness in Nature as a Path of Self-Discovery*, New World Library, Novato, CA 2006.

Conze, Edward, trans., *The Buddha's Law amongst the Birds*, Bruno Cassirer, Oxford 1955.

Dillard, Annie, 'Pilgrim at Tinker Creek' and 'Living like weasels', in *The Annie Dillard Reader*, Harper Perennial, New York 1995.

Emerson, Ralph Waldo, *Selected Essays*, Penguin, New York 1985.

Bibliography

Gros, Frédéric, *A Philosophy of Walking*, Verso, London 2014.

Haight, Gordon, *George Eliot: A Biography*, Penguin, New York 1985.

Hass, Robert, *The Essential Haiku: Versions of Basho, Buson, and Issa*, Bloodaxe Books, Tarset 2013.

Horner, I.B., trans., *Cullavagga*, in *The Book of the Discipline (Vinaya Pitaka)*, vol.5, Pali Text Society, Oxford 1992, section 7, pp.272–4.

Hughes, Ted, *Collected Poems*, Farrar, Straus and Giroux, New York 2003.

Hughes, Ted, *The Hawk in the Rain*, Faber and Faber, London 1986.

Hughes, Ted, *Moortown Diary*, Faber and Faber, London, 1989.

Hughes, Ted, *Poetry in the Making: A Handbook for Writing*, Faber and Faber, London 2008.

Ireland, John D., trans., *The Udana and the Itivuttaka*, Buddhist Publication Society, Kandy 1997.

Kamala Tiyavanich, *Forest Recollections: Wandering Monks in Twentieth-Century Thailand*, University of Hawai'i Press, Honolulu 1997.

Lawrence, D.H., *Birds, Beasts, and Flowers*, Penguin, London 1999.

Linzey, Andrew, *Why Animal Suffering Matters: Philosophy, Theology, and Practical Ethics*, Oxford University Press, New York 2009.

Louv, Richard, *Last Child in the Woods: Saving Our Children from Nature-Deficit Disorder*, Atlantic Books, London 2010.

Mabey, Richard, *Beechcombings: The Narrative of Trees*, Chatto & Windus, London 2007.

Mabey, Richard, *Nature Cure*, Vintage, London 2008.

Macfarlane, Robert, *Mountains of the Mind: A History of a Fascination*, Granta, London 2008.

Macfarlane, Robert, *The Old Ways: A Journey on Foot*, Penguin, London 2012.

Macfarlane, Robert, *Wild Places*, Granta, London 2008.

MacNeice, Louis, *Collected Poems*, Faber and Faber, London 2002.

Maitland, Sara, *A Book of Silence*, Granta, London 2009.

Bibliography

McMahan, David L., *The Making of Buddhist Modernism*, Oxford University Press, New York 2008.

Monbiot, George, *Feral: Rewilding the Sea, Land, and Human Life*, Penguin, London 2014.

Nanamoli, Bhikkhu, and Bhikkhu Bodhi, trans., *Majjhima Nikaya*, Wisdom Publications, Somerville, MA 2005.

Rackham, Oliver, *The Making of the English Countryside*, Weidenfeld & Nicolson, London 1995.

Ratnaguna, *The Art of Reflection*, Windhorse Publications, Cambridge 2010.

Redgrove, Peter, *The Black Goddess and the Sixth Sense*, Paladin, London 1989.

Ryan, P.D., *Buddhism and the Natural World: Towards a Meaningful Myth*, Windhorse Publications, Birmingham 1998.

Sangharakshita, *Living with Awareness: A Guide to the Satipatthana Sutta*, Windhorse Publications, Birmingham 2003.

Sangharakshita, *Puja: The Triratna Book of Devotional Texts*, Windhorse Publications, Cambridge 2008.

Sangharakshita, *The Yogi's Joy: Songs of Milarepa*, Windhorse Publications, Birmingham 2006.

Sarvananda, *Solitude and Loneliness: A Buddhist View*, Windhorse Publications, Cambridge 2012.

Shepherd, Nan, *The Living Mountain*, in *The Grampian Quartet*, Canongate, Edinburgh 1996.

Storr, Anthony, *Solitude*, Collins, London 1989.

Thoreau, Henry David, *Walden: or, Life in the Woods*, Dover Publications, New York 1995.

Tomkies, Mike, *A Last Wild Place*, Jonathan Cape, London 1984.

WINDHORSE PUBLICATIONS

Windhorse Publications is a Buddhist charitable company based in the UK. We place great emphasis on producing books of high quality that are accessible and relevant to those interested in Buddhism at whatever level. We are the main publisher of the works of Sangharakshita, the founder of the Triratna Buddhist Order and Community. Our books draw on the whole range of the Buddhist tradition, including translations of traditional texts, commentaries, books that make links with contemporary culture and ways of life, biographies of Buddhists, and works on meditation.

As a not-for-profit enterprise, we ensure that all surplus income is invested in new books and improved production methods, to better communicate Buddhism in the 21st century. We welcome donations to help us continue our work – to find out more, go to windhorsepublications.com.

The Windhorse is a mythical animal that flies over the earth carrying on its back three precious jewels, bringing these invaluable gifts to all humanity: the Buddha (the 'awakened one'), his teaching, and the community of all his followers.

Windhorse Publications
169 Mill Road
Cambridge CB1 3AN
UK
info@windhorsepublications.com

Perseus Distribution
210 American Drive
Jackson TN 38301
USA

Windhorse Books
PO Box 574
Newtown NSW 2042
Australia

THE TRIRATNA BUDDHIST COMMUNITY

Windhorse Publications is a part of the Triratna Buddhist Community, an international movement with centres in Europe, India, North and South America and Australasia. At these centres, members of the Triratna Buddhist Order offer classes in meditation and Buddhism. Activities of the Triratna Community also include retreat centres, residential spiritual communities, ethical Right Livelihood businesses, and the Karuna Trust, a UK fundraising charity that supports social welfare projects in the slums and villages of India.

Through these and other activities, Triratna is developing a unique approach to Buddhism, not simply as a philosophy and a set of techniques, but as a creatively directed way of life for all people living in the conditions of the modern world.

If you would like more information about Triratna please visit thebuddhistcentre.com or write to:

London Buddhist Centre
51 Roman Road
London E2 0HU
UK

Aryaloka
14 Heartwood Circle
Newmarket NH 03857
USA

Sydney Buddhist Centre
24 Enmore Road
Sydney NSW 2042
Australia

ALSO BY VAJRAGUPTA
Buddhism: Tools for Living Your Life

In this guide for all those seeking a meaningful spiritual path, Vajragupta provides clear explanations of the main Buddhist teachings, as well as a variety of exercises designed to help readers develop or deepen their practice.

Appealing, readable, and practical, blending accessible teachings, practices, and personal stories . . . as directly relevant to modern life as it is comprehensive and rigorous. – Tricycle: The Buddhist Review, 2007

I'm very pleased that someone has finally written this book! At last, a real 'toolkit' for living a Buddhist life, his practical suggestions are hard to resist! – Saddhanandi, Director of Adhisthana

ISBN 9781 899579 74 7
£11.99 / $18.95 / €17.95
192 pages

Sailing the Worldly Winds: A Buddhist Way through the Ups and Downs of Life

How do we really get on in this world? Tossed around by gain, buffeted by loss, borne aloft by praise, cast down by blame, how can we not be ground under, lose all direction, confidence, and sense of purpose? The Buddha had clear guidance on how to rise above these 'worldly winds', and Vajragupta here opens up for us the Buddha's compassionate yet uncompromising teaching.

Using reflections, exercises and suggestions for daily practice, this book can help you find greater equanimity and perspective in the ups and downs – big and small – of everyday life.

ISBN 978 1 9073141 0 0
£5.99 / $8.95 /€8.95
128 pages

Not About Being Good: A Practical Guide to Buddhist Ethics

Subhadramati

While there are numerous books on Buddhist meditation and philosophy, there are few books that are entirely devoted to the practice of Buddhist ethics. Subhadramati communicates clearly both their founding principles and the practical methods to embody them.

Buddhist ethics are not about conforming to a set of conventions, not about 'being good' in order to gain rewards. Instead, living ethically springs from the awareness that other people are no different from yourself. You can actively develop this awareness, through cultivating love, clarity and contentment. Helping you to come into greater harmony with all that lives, this is ultimately your guidebook to a more satisfactory life.

ISBN 9781 909314 01 6
£9.99 / $16.95 / €12.95
176 pages

Change Your Mind

Paramananda

An accessible and thorough guide, this best-seller introduces two Buddhist meditations and deals imaginatively with practical difficulties, meeting distraction and doubt with determination and humour.

Inspiring, calming and friendly ... If you've always thought meditation might be a good idea, but found other step-by-step guides lacking in spirit, this book could finally get you going. – Here's Health

ISBN 9781 899579 75 4
£9.99 / $13.95 / €12.95
208 pages

The Buddha on Wall Street: What's Wrong with Capitalism and What We Can Do about It

Vaḍḍhaka Linn

After his Enlightenment the Buddha set out to help liberate the individual, and create a society free from suffering. The economic resources now exist to offer a realistic possibility of providing everyone with decent food, shelter, work and leisure, to allow each of us to fulfil our potential as human beings, whilst protecting the environment. What is it in the nature of modern capitalism which prevents that happening? Can Buddhism help us build something better than our current economic system, to reduce suffering and help the individual to freedom? In this thought-provoking work, Vaḍḍhaka Linn explores answers to these questions by examining our economic world from the moral standpoint established by the Buddha.

An original, insightful, and provocative evaluation of our economic situation today. If you wonder about the social implications of Buddhist teachings, this is an essential book. – David Loy, author *Money, Sex, War, Karma*

Lays bare the pernicious consequences of corporate capitalism and draws forth from Buddhism suggestions for creating benign alternatives conducive to true human flourishing. – Bhikkhu Bodhi, editor *In the Buddha's Words*

Questions any definition of wellbeing that does not rest on a firm ethical foundation, developing a refreshing Buddhist critique of the ends of economic activity. – Dominic Houlder, Adjunct Professor in Strategy and Entrepreneurship, London Business School

ISBN 978 1 909314 44 3
£9.99 / $16.99 / €12.95
272 pages

Mindful Emotion: a short course in kindness

Dr Paramabandhu Groves and Dr Jed Shamel

This book is all about kindness behaviour training (KBT). The authors have drawn on their clinical experience as well as Buddhism to develop a practical course in cultivating kindness, intended to complement and augment other mindfulness-based approaches.

A range of psychological theories and areas of research inform the KBT approach, primarily findings from cognitive neuroscience, as well as evolutionary and positive psychology literatures. It also uses a range of exercises found to be helpful in Eastern traditions, such as Buddhism. The KBT exercises have been isolated from their religious or spiritual origins and are used on a secular basis.

A stimulating guide and training program that uses the analogy of cultivating a garden that results in the finest flowers and fruits to illustrate the process of cultivating kindness toward others . . . . what our world so badly needs right now. – Bhikshuni Thubten Chodron

Buy this book, read it, practise with it. It's a wonderfully welcome addition to the body of work around mindfulness and compassion. I'll certainly be recommending it to all those who have attended my mindfulness classes. – Michael Chaskalson, author of *Mindfulness in Eight Weeks*

ISBN 978 1 909314 70 2
£11.99 / $18.95 / €14.95
240 pages